Verdandi

Executing strategic change is about growing a business, cutting costs, fixing infrastructure and reducing exposure to risk. Verdandi transfers expert knowledge to people so they can drive successful change programmes and projects.

Successful Project Management

Verdandi's complete framework for managing change - from idea to benefit realisation – is built around Successful Project Management™ methodology, adopted by major UK companies as their corporate standard.

Since 1984, Verdandi has delivered over 2,000 significant change programmes and projects for more than 200 clients using the methodology, and trained over 10,000 client employees in the principles and practices, which they continue to use to deliver beneficial change.

Successful Project Management methodology was devised in 1974 to control the delivery of projects within the industrial products division of Burmah Castrol.

> **Successful Project Management is the pragmatic application of a system of principles, processes, guidelines, tools and techniques to define, plan and deliver beneficial change.**

It works on original principles, using simple and effective processes that focus on the people aspects of projects to achieve exceptional results.

To be successful, the objectives and scope of any project must be clearly defined, and the deliverables agreed. Three lists are then needed:

- A meticulous and logically sequenced plan, built around deliverables, for things you can do – Tasks & Activities

- A list of unexpected circumstances and refuted assumptions that will cause slippage to current or imminent events unless they can be resolved - Issues

- A list of the adverse outcomes of future events which are subject to chance - Risks'.

Activities state what has to be done, by whom, by when, using what resource, bound by a negotiated delivery 'promise' - people care about their promises and will routinely deliver unless they encounter an issue.

When an issue surfaces, it is immediately escalated by the Project Leader to the person empowered to answer it. A resolution is swiftly agreed and communicated to the team. If intransigence is encountered, and slippage is threatened, the issue is broadcast to the sponsors and stakeholders.

A risk is mitigated or avoided but if significant risk remains a contingency plan is created. If the adverse outcome occurs, the contingency plan is used.

When handed over, a key deliverable must enable the customer to realise the anticipated benefits.

The methodology has evolved significantly but the original principles remain the heartbeat.

Handbook

This Handbook is a reference guide to Successful Project Management™ methodology. It explains how to manage projects that change the business-as-usual activities of an organisation within agreed quality, specification, time, and resource targets, so that the anticipated benefits can be realised or exceeded.

This handbook provides:

- A description of the business-as-usual and change environments of an organisation
- A view of how to run projects within the context of the overall change environment
- Step by step guidelines for the holder of any project-related role
- Identified tools and techniques that can be applied within a project environment as and when required.

Tools are identified in this Handbook with blue type.

Project Toolkit™

The fully integrated set of tools described in this handbook for use with Successful Project Management™ – Project Toolkit™ - can be obtained as Microsoft Word and Excel templates.

Project Toolkit™ is distributed under licence and can be:

- Provided on a CD for loading on your corporate intranet
- Accessed via the Web using a password

Please contact us for more information about Project Toolkit™ or for details of the other toolkits we provide for value, resource and programme management.

Learning

Verdandi provides a full range of high-impact courses and events designed to help you develop your project management capability and extend your skills.

Foundation Training	Sponsoring Strategic Change	½ day
	Applying Programme Management	3 days
	Sponsoring Successful Projects	½ day
	Leading Successful Projects	2 days
	Working in a Project Environment	1 day
	Introduction to Project Management	1 day
Accelerated Learning	Partnering	per day
	Master Classes	2 hours
	Skill Boosts	2 hours
	Coaching & Mentoring	per day

Details can be found on our website at www.verdandi.co.uk

Copyright

This handbook contains proprietary information that is the confidential property of Verdandi Limited and is for use only by the intended recipient or entity. Use by any other person or entity is strictly forbidden.

This document may not be reproduced, copied, disclosed or otherwise made available to any person or entity except as expressly authorised in writing by Verdandi Limited.

First published 1984, new edition 2008, latest edition 2010.

ISBN 978-1-906169-38-1

Successful Project Management™, the SPM motif, Project Toolkit™ and motif are registered trademarks of Verdandi Limited.

Contents

Contents

The Organisation

Goal

The goal of any organisation is to increase its value to those who have a stake in its success.

> **The term 'organisation' describes any public or private limited company, any agency or established body of national or local government, any partnership, trust or charity.**

Those who have a stake, be they individuals or a group of people, want to receive real value, in the form of measurable financial or non-financial benefits in return for the resources they put in. These individuals and groups may include directors, employees, customers, suppliers, shareholders, partners, investors, regulators, and other third parties.

Strategy

Most organisations have a coherent strategy and business plan – many have a Target Operating Model.

A Target Operating Model is a set of charts that define the future business and technical capabilities of the organisation, and are used to guide its development.

Organisations perform best when people understand the strategic context of their work.

Communicating the strategy in a form that can be understood and supported by the people responsible for, and impacted by strategic change, helps everyone participate more effectively in the development of the business.

> **A Strategic Vision document is used to form the links between the strategy, Target Operating Model and Customer Value Proposition, and communicate the needed outcomes.**

A Strategic Vision document can be used to:

- Identify gaps in capability and thinking
- Achieve organisational focus and buy-in
- Identify the projects that will deliver the strategy and business plan
- Create a clear context for the planning and realisation of benefits.

Work

Work is carried out within the organisation to achieve an increase in value. This work is either business-as-usual or change.

Business-as-usual

Business-as-usual is the day-to-day operations of an organisation, carried out by its existing domain structure, and the main way that any organisation increases its value.

> *The term 'domain' describes a distinct, self-managed business unit, function, or area of expertise that adapts to meet changing needs and demands, the performance of which is measured.*

These day-to-day operations are:

- Triggered by a customer transaction or event
- Carried out following a process or formula
- Value-adding to internal and external customers.

The customer may be the general public buying products or services, or another domain requiring a service, either from within or outside the organisation.

Some processes and formulae may be commonplace in an industry - others will be unique to the organisation. Processes are automated by systems to make them efficient and effective.

The efficiency and effectiveness of each process is vital to the success of the organisation.

Key performance indicators and critical success factors, often included in a balanced scorecard, highlight the need for improved performance, and are a main focus for executive directors.

> *A 'key performance indicator' is a measurable parameter, relevant to the organisation, which can be used to monitor progress towards its goal.*
>
> *A 'critical success factor' is a significant entity to which achievement of objectives and realisation of benefits is critical, and which must be within limits in order to achieve success.*

Change

A change is an event used to alter favourably the state of something. It involves creating, integrating or transforming the capabilities, enablers and assets of an organisation, which include people, processes and systems.

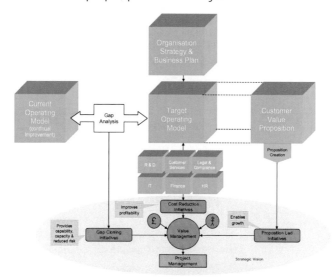

Figure 1: Sources of Change

One of the following will trigger an idea for change:

- A need to create a new or improved value proposition to grow the organisation

- A need to remove waste and so reduce the cost of delivering or servicing the Customer Value Proposition

- A need for additional or different infrastructure that creates the capability or capacity for processing increased business

- A need to reduce exposure to risk.

Continual Improvement

Continual improvement is used to achieve incremental improvements to business performance where it:

- Requires no significant intra-domain cooperation

- Uses few resources

- Can be authorised without referral – normally because the manager responsible for the process is responsible for the budget.

Business-as-usual includes small changes and improvements, executed using 'continual improvement' techniques.

Initiative

When continual improvement cannot realise the needed benefits there must be an initiative - work that creates new, improves existing or eliminates unwanted business-as-usual, and realises significant benefits that add to the value of the organisation.

An initiative:

- Contributes to the organisation's strategy and business plan

- Requires resources or intra-domain cooperation beyond any one person's or team's limits of authority

- Has a specified beginning and end

- Realises measurable benefits

- Is delivered by projects and programmes.

Project

A project is work that changes or determines the path to change business-as-usual which includes:

- Definition and agreement of the objectives and scope of the work

- Specification of the deliverables, and their associated quality standards, that constitute the change

- Planning the work of supplier and customer domains to make and implement these deliverables

- Managing the issues and risks inherent in making the change

- Validation and agreement of the costs and benefits

- Management of change requests

- Ensuring that all deliverables are created in a quality manner, on time and within budget to enable the anticipated benefits to be realised.

Programme

A programme is work that delivers large-scale change to business-as-usual through the coordination of a coherent set of projects. It may:

- Involve complex supplier and customer relationships, and deliverables
- Carry significant business risk and be sensitive to many factors
- Require business-wide commitment and persistence to succeed
- Realise benefits in many domains
- Be of long duration – usually greater than one year.

The suggested reasons for a programme are:

- The amount of planning is too much for one Project Leader
- The work is more easily delivered and the risk level reduced if it is managed as a set of tightly co-ordinated projects
- There is a high degree of interdependency between a number of related projects
- There are many domains involved.

At the top end of the programme scale are strategic programmes, which implement a significant part of the organisation strategy. They're complex and critical to the success of the organisation, and an executive director is usually the sponsor.

In any organisation there will exist an environment for business-as-usual and an environment for change.

Business-as-usual Environment

Within an organisation there are many 'domains'. Within each domain there may be several subordinate domains, and so on.

Within each domain, teams composed of one or more people do work. Each domain has a manager and each team a leader.

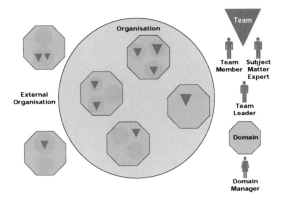

Figure 2: The Business-as-usual Environment

No organisation exists in isolation - it has to deal daily with customers, suppliers, regulators and so on, which are organisations in their own right. Therefore, the business-as-usual environment of an organisation extends beyond its own boundaries to include these external domains.

It is the business-as-usual environment and its processes, people and systems which is incrementally improved using continual improvement and changed using projects. The same people who carry out the business-as-usual processes, do the continual improvement work, and are involved in the delivery of projects.

Domain Manager

The domain manager is responsible for the business performance of the domain, including:

- Negotiating its budget, headcount, facilities, and performance targets
- Managing the operation of the domain so that it achieves its performance targets.

A domain manager organises the domain to include other subordinate domains or teams. One or more teams carry out the business-as-usual processes.

> *A team is a group of people within a domain accountable for specific business-as-usual work for which the Domain Manager is responsible.*

Team Leader

A Team Leader is responsible for the operational performance of the team, as required by the domain manager, including:

- Operation of the team
- Negotiation of its targets
- Development of the team.

A Team Leader is accountable for the completion of all the agreed work by the team, by negotiated dates, using agreed human and financial resources, to the agreed specifications and quality standards.

The work is carried out or completed by team members.

Team Member

A team member is a person within a team who is responsible for doing work as directed by the team leader. They are recruited and retained for personal knowledge, skills and experience.

A team member may have special knowledge, skills or experience that, for a particular work-assignment, puts the team member into the role of subject matter expert.

Subject Matter Expert

A subject matter expert can:

- Explain complex or specialist processes and entities, in terms that non-specialists can understand
- Lead co-workers in the application of the processes and creation of the entities

The non-routine work of team members is usually centered around a subject matter expert.

Change Environment

For every organisation pursuing its strategic vision, creating the right environment for the realisation of benefits from change is mission critical.

In the change environment, a change framework has a similar purpose and value for an organisation to that which an operating system has for a computer. In a computer, transactions are the driver. The operating system orchestrates the hardware components to work with the applications and database so as to realise valuable outcomes.

In an organisation, ideas are the driver. The change framework orchestrates business-as-usual to work with initiatives and knowledge so as to realise value from change.

A change framework has five capabilities. As well as the capability to create a strategic vision it has:

*   Value Management
*   Resource Management
*   Programme Management
*   Project Management

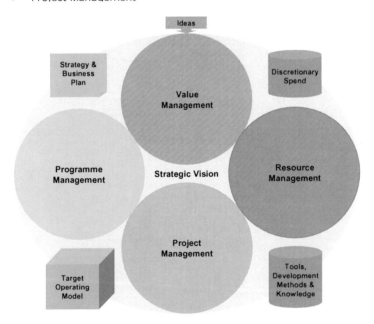

Figure 3: Change Framework

© Verdandi Limited 1984-2010

Value Management

No organisation can afford to spend money on the wrong ideas, or invest in the right ideas without getting the full benefits in return.

People work more effectively when they know that they are working on ideas that contribute to the organisation's success and will be carried through to produce value. People are frustrated when their work is wasted.

Executive management will know how much discretionary spend is available to drive the organisation forward from where it is today, to where they want it to be in the future.

It will not be able to afford to implement all its ideas - some will not even work. Ideas should be considered just as an investment banker would pick winning investments, quickly re-scoping or terminating those that do not demonstrate an adequate return at acceptable risk, prior to major investment - pushing forward with new ideas.

> *Value Management is the policies, processes, standards and practices that enable the investment in initiatives to be governed effectively and ensure consistent worth to the organisation.*

Benefits from change are both financial and non-financial. Every project must enable benefits to be realised but not every project will realise financial benefits. The organisation will welcome non-financial benefits, providing they are ones which it is specifically seeking.

Value Management creates an environment to manage the organisation's portfolio of projects, establish financial governance and realise benefits in line with the strategy and business plan.

Resource Management

Regulating the flow of projects in order to challenge, but not overwhelm people, is essential. If projects are allowed to flow freely into an organisation, available resources become swamped. When this happens, activity increases but, very quickly, productivity declines, rate of progress slows, and the capacity for delivering change actually diminishes.

> *Resource Management is the policies, processes, standards and practices that enable the resources of an organisation to be optimally deployed so that more can be accomplished with less resource.*

Resource Management means:

- Harnessing and leveraging the available resources from across the organisation
- Having a simple, consistent and business-wide approach that allows critical resource information to be extracted for effective decision making
- Actively managing interdependencies and capacity pinchpoints to enable the throughput of projects to be governed
- Establishing a fulfilment capability that ensures optimal deployment of skilled resources to an affordable, feasible and viable change plan
- Aligning future resource levels and developing skills to meet expected demand

Regulating the flow of projects to challenge available resources rather than swamping them, allows people the time to rise to the challenge and perform more effectively.

Value and resource management operate together as one end-to-end, 'change planning' process.

Programme Management

> **Programme Management is the agile and adaptable application of a set of processes, tools, techniques and behaviours to define, plan, and deliver large-scale, beneficial change to an organisation.**

Programme Management enables an organisation to deliver complex, large-scale change in order to achieve part of the strategy and business plan. Due to their size and complexity, programmes must deliver change through a coherent set of projects.

Programmes include processes that:

- Gain the commitment of the executive board to the strategic vision, with each board member advocating the change and when called upon becoming accountable for benefit realisation
- Identify and appoint the best people to lead and deliver the programme and each constituent project
- Communicate the programme vision and objectives effectively to impacted people at all levels
- Segment the programme into manageable projects that will deliver the programme by the required deadline
- Encourage, enthuse and rally people to undertake programme related work, often in parallel with their day jobs, during a period when people are faced with uncertainty, and perhaps critical changes in responsibilities
- Adapt the programme to changing circumstances
- Realise the benefits visualised at the outset.

Project Management

> **Project Management is the pragmatic application of
> a set of processes, tools, techniques and behaviours
> to deliver a beneficial change to an organisation.**

Project Management involves the definition, planning and control of
human, financial, material and knowledge resources; to complete
the project work successfully, and so enable the realisation of
anticipated benefits.

A successful project is one that completes the work to specifications
and quality standards within all financial, manpower and time
targets, and achieves its stated objectives.

*Programme and project management are the delivery 'vehicles' of
beneficial change.*

What is Successful Project Management?

Successful Project Management is an agile and flexible project management methodology aimed at realising benefit from change.

> *A methodology is a system of principles, processes, guidelines, tools and techniques that describe both 'what has to be done' and 'how to do it'.*

It is made up of precisely defined roles, clearly illustrated processes supported by a project toolkit and comprehensive glossary.

> *Successful Project Management™ enables Project Leaders to drive quality project delivery at maximum speed and minimum cost, and with less risk so that the Business Owner and Executive Sponsor can drive the realisation of benefits with confidence.*

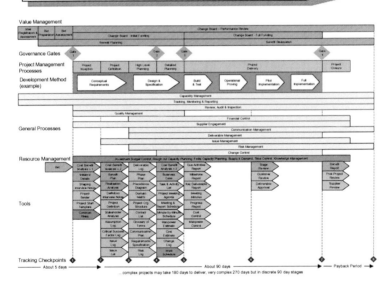

Figure 4: Successful Project Management - Schema

Using a methodology makes it easier for people to work together to deliver projects so that anticipated benefits can be realised or exceeded. It comprises a set of guidelines that anyone can adapt to the needs of any project.

Successful Project Management has six core 'project management processes', shown above in peach, supported by eleven 'general processes', common to both project and programme management, shown in yellow. Six general processes are used in standard form, see Figure 5 below, the other five are specific to each organisation. The tools used in project management are illustrated in Figure 4.

There are strong linkages between the core project management processes and Benefit Planning, Benefit Realisation, and Knowledge Management. Together they form the 'mechanics'.

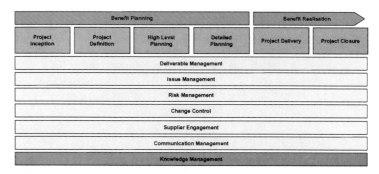

Figure 5: Successful Project Management 'mechanics'

Using Successful Project Management, the Project Leader achieves success by working with supplier and customer domains to:

- Identify and specify all required deliverables and associated quality standards
- Agree the manpower and cost need to make and implement these deliverables
- Plan and schedule the work of creating these deliverables
- Ensure the creation of these deliverables to agreed quality, on time, using only the agreed resources.

Application of these processes – the art – ensures success by:

- Managing people's expectations
- Valuing people and treating them as professionals
- Negotiating and managing delivery promises
- Resolving issues in an assertive but non-confrontational way.

Development Methods

Very few projects genuinely pioneer and it's probable that what a project is about to do has been done successfully by someone, somewhere, before.

Suppliers and subject matter experts often document their best practice way of creating a complex deliverable to give them a professional 'edge' – these are referred to as 'development methods'. Following a proven path saves money, reduces risk and speeds progress to quality delivery.

> *A development method is a documented, systematic and proven way of completing work, used to guide the efficient creation of a complex deliverable. It:*
>
> - *Illustrates the major stepping stones involved in achieving the outcome*
>
> - *Defines the processes and interfaces between processes*
>
> - *Identifies the deliverables, materials, equipment and quality standards*

A development method is required for each complex deliverable. Development methods are obtained from internal and external suppliers and applied using Successful Project Management.

Management Control

> *An organisation's project portfolio is its record of all registered initiatives aimed at implementing the strategy and business plan in line with its Target Operating Model, each of which realises needed benefit.*

Management of the project portfolio is the responsibility of the Head of Change, perhaps supported by a Head of Demand and a Head of Supply - see Change Environment Structure. Governance is the responsibility of the Change Board.

Change Board

> *The Change Board is a panel of Executive Sponsors, chaired by a senior executive, who together are responsible for the realisation of benefits from the organisation's project portfolio.*

The Change Board is accountable to the executive board. Responsibilities include:

- Agreeing the balance and blend of the project portfolio

- Authorising initiatives that will deliver the strategy and business plan

- Approving initial and full funding of programmes, and projects

- Monitoring status and progress, giving direction where appropriate

- Monitoring the realisation of benefit from programmes, projects and continual improvement.

An effective Change Board operates with a benefit-focused agenda and has 'cabinet responsibility' for delivery of targeted value from an agreed amount of investment.

With a regular focus, programmes and projects that cannot demonstrate alignment with the strategy and Target Operating Model, or deliver the required benefits are quickly terminated to avoid wasted investment.

This places executives in control of both the discretionary spend and accrual of benefits.

Governance Gates

There are two types of checkpoint that, together with progress and status reporting, enable the Change Board to maintain effective control over a project portfolio.

> *Governance gates are points in a programme or project where feasibility and viability is reviewed, and executive approval is needed before it can proceed beyond that point.*

There are four governance gates:

1   Bid Assessment - The point at which initial funding is granted or denied by the Change Board – some preparatory design or development work may begin whilst the project is incepted and planned

2   Feasibility & Viability – The point at which objectives and scope have been defined, the benefits confirmed, and the project planned to a level of confidence such that the Executive Sponsor can decide to proceed, re-scope or terminate

3   Full Funding Approval – The point at which the Cost Benefit Analysis has been substantiated through detailed planning so that a decision can be taken by the Change Board to proceed, re-scope or terminate

4   Closure Approval – The point at which the Change Board agree that the project can end and the budgets close; the Business Owner remains responsible to the Change Board for benefit realisation and risk management.

Terminating a project, which is neither feasible nor viable, is a sign of strength, and the earlier this is done the less investment is wasted.

Tracking Checkpoints

> *Tracking checkpoints are dates at which progress is checked to confirm that definition and planning is proceeding to a pre-agreed timetable.*

There are eight checkpoints, monitored by the Change Office, four of which coincide with governance gates, see Figure 4.

Change Office

> *The Change Office is the team who support the change planning and change delivery processes across the organisation.*

Responsibilities of the Change Office include:

- Expediting the processing of ideas and coordination of facilitation services
- Scheduling planned resources to programmes and projects
- Supporting the inception, delivery and closure of programmes and projects
- Monitoring the effective use and utilisation of resources
- Maintaining policies, methods, standards, libraries and the Project Community Website
- Gathering and collating management information
- Tracking and expediting progress of programmes and projects
- Preparing and circulating progress, status and performance reports
- Managing the acquisition, storage and retrieval of knowledge.

Knowledge Library

> *A Knowledge Library is an organised store of intellectual assets, managed by the Change Office and available to all people doing initiative-related work.*

A Knowledge Library typically contains:

- Tools
- Development methods
- Quality standards
- Project plans from past projects
- Common risks
- Re-usable components.

The library is continually added to by people within the project community and made accessible via the intranet, so enabling knowledge to be accessed where and when needed for the benefit of the organisation.

What does it take?

Project Duration

> *The only reliable way to achieve project success is to plan the work – then to work the project plan.*

Typically, having incepted a project, the first 20% of the elapsed time is spent defining objectives and scope, and in planning. The remaining 80% is spent delivering and closing the project. See Figure 6.

Figure 6: Project Duration

If, for example, Project Delivery is expected to take place over a period of 90 elapsed days, definition and planning will take about 18 elapsed days.

In practice, the challenge is often to achieve difficult project deadlines. Flexibility and measured risk taking is usually required to meet the project objectives. For example, to gain time, the Project Sponsor might agree with subject matter experts to take the risk of starting Project Delivery activities before Project Inception and wait for project management to catch up and take over.

Conversely, some projects will include deliverables the creation of which take a fixed length of time regardless of the amount of effort applied; or may have the project work scheduled over a longer period than necessary to fit in with interdependencies with other initiatives.

Project Management Effort

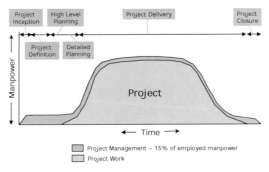

Figure 7: Project Management Effort

As a guideline, for every 100 man-days of project work, approximately 15 man-days of project management effort are required. Of that effort, as a guideline:

- **Inception** - Typically requires 1-2 days effort from the Project Leader

- **Definition** - Unless the project is especially complex, or the Project Leader and Project Partner are inexperienced, allow ½ man-day of effort for interviews with the Project Sponsor and each Project Stakeholder, and add a further 2 man-days for the preparation of a Project Definition document; the period over which this is done depends entirely on people's availability

- **Planning** - For every 100 man-days of project work, approximately 6 man-days of Project Leader, Project Partner and Project Team Member effort will be required for planning; the split between High Level Planning and Detailed Planning depends on the number of deliverables, and the number of supplier and customer domains

- **Delivery** - For every 100 man-days of project work, approximately 7 man-days of control effort will be required dealing with issues, risks, changes and reporting

- **Closure** - About 4 days, is usually needed.

In determining the effort required for project management, take into account the:

- Combined knowledge, skill and experience of the Project Leader and Project Partner

- Size and complexity of the project.

- Amount of manpower needed to do the project work

- Experience of the suppliers

What is a Project Leader?

In organisations, the ability to lead projects successfully is a necessary management discipline. A Project Leader's role is to deliver successful projects. To do this, Project Leaders must adapt rapidly to conflicting pressures, unexpected circumstances and changing requirements - to get the project completed and so enable benefits to be realised.

> *Leadership is a function of knowing yourself, having a vision that is well communicated, building trust among colleagues and taking effective action.*

The Project Leader must use judgement in the selection of tools that are adequate for the planning and control, apply project management processes pragmatically and employ appropriate techniques to motivate people to take on essential roles, and responsibilities. It requires:

- Focus - taking responsibility for successful project delivery
- Delegation – empowering and trusting people to complete work
- Persistence - coaching and mentoring people to achieve results that may be outside of their comfort zone
- Dedication - doing whatever is necessary to succeed – leading projects is not a 9-5 job
- Credibility - earning the respect of all involved parties.

To deliver project success, Project Leaders need key competencies, skills, styles, knowledge and experience.

Key Competencies

A key competency is a set of behaviours associated with high performance in a particular role. Project Leader key competencies are:

Key Competency	Description
Customer empathy	Placing the customer in the forefront of your thinking and demonstrating this by words and actions
Influential communication	Conveying impact and credibility in interpersonal situations
Work orchestration	Consulting and giving direction to multi-functional project teams
Personal drive and confidence	Being positive, enthusiastic and focused
Team leadership and development	Providing direction and support to promote effective individual, and team working
Analytical reasoning	Using analytical and conceptual problem solving skills to understand complex information

Skills

A skill is a special ability to do something. Project Leader skills include:

Skill	Description
Facilitation	Assisting in the progress of work by other people
Interpersonal communication	Creating an efficient and effective channel of communications between two people
Interviewing	Assembling an agreed set of information from the communication and exchange of information on a specific topic
Listening	Hearing and interpreting what another means, implies and intends by what they say or do
Marketing	Disseminating information to ensure that all relevant people are aware of opportunities, progress and achievement
Negotiating	Reaching an agreement with another person by a give and take process such that each person is content with the outcome, and committed to the delivery of the given promises
Organising	Establishing and maintaining structures - people, equipment, services, materials, finances, knowledge - that enable, and support processes
Planning	Formulating, at an appropriate level of detail, what has to be done, to what methods and quality standards, how it will be achieved, by when and by whom, using what manpower and money
Problem solving	Overcoming difficulties caused by people whose actions or behaviour is having a negative impact
Public relations	Presenting a situation so that people have the most favourable perception
Selling	Identifying benefits others want to achieve, the needs they are trying to satisfy and matching these expectations with what is affordable
Time management	Making the best use of one's own and others' time to complete all work commitments

Styles

Behaviours adopted to achieve an intended outcome.

Style	Description
Mentor	Giving direct advice, when invited, by asking questions that improve a person's skills and abilities
Consultant	Giving of advice on specialist subjects, the way an organisation works or the politics of an organisation
Supporter	Providing services and assistance to those doing work or dealing with a difficulty
Coach	Interacting with another in a particular context that results in improving the future for the other person
'Obstacle remover'	Taking action to enable someone to make progress in the completion of work
'Ankle biter'	Unremittingly but fairly driving someone who has work to complete

Knowledge

Knowledge is what is known by people and possessed by the organisation that enables constructive activity. Project Leader knowledge includes the:

- Understanding of project management – the processes, tools and techniques

- Appreciation of, or the ability to quickly assimilate, the subject matter of a project, grasp the fundamentals and put expertise to effective use

- Understanding of people behaviours.

Experience

Experience is direct know-how or ability within a discipline gained over time by personal practice.

It takes time to acquire project leadership experience. Good Project Leaders are always seeking new projects in which they can gain more experience - they never stop learning.

Who does what?

Project Organisation

Figure 8 shows the organisational structure of the roles involved in a project.

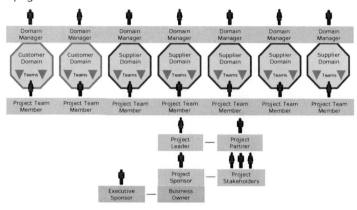

Figure 8: Project Organisation Structure

> *A role is a set of responsibilities and accountabilities accepted by a person for a limited duration, which requires some or all of the person's time.*

Project roles may be full or part-time and are for the duration of the project only. It is not uncommon for one person to hold more than one role in the same project – and, indeed, to hold roles in several projects at the same time.

Executive Sponsor

The Executive Sponsor is accountable for the strategy and business plan, and takes responsibility for part of the project portfolio with a focus on the realisation of benefits.

Business Owner

The Business Owner is responsible for championing an idea from its first identification to the realisation of all its planned benefits - as Project Sponsor they are responsible, through stakeholder management, for the success of the project.

Project Sponsor

Project Sponsor is the role is held by the Business Owner for the duration of the project. Responsibilities include:

- Selecting, appointing, empowering and supporting the Project Leader and Project Partner
- Identifying Project Stakeholders
- Articulating and advocating the project vision
- Deciding the project's objectives and scope.

> *A Project Sponsor must be active and involved in the management of the project. If the Project Sponsor is unable to fulfil the responsibilities of the role, an issue should be escalated to the Executive Sponsor.*

Project Stakeholder

A Project Stakeholder is a manager of a large domain who has a vested interest in the outcome of the project, can influence the Project Sponsor, whose cooperation is necessary for project success and whose responsibilities are:

- Representing the interests of own domain
- Influencing the project's vision, objectives and scope
- Identifying and validating benefits
- Advocating the project.

> *It is better to have too many Project Stakeholders than too few – ignoring the views and requirements of influential people is unwise.*
>
> *It's almost certainly worth having every customer domain represented by a Project Stakeholder.*

Project Leader

The Project Leader is responsible for successful delivery of the project, working with the Project Partner. Responsibilities are:

- Preparing project documentation
- Planning the project with experts from customer and supplier domains
- Organising required resources

- Managing changes to the project
- Leading the Project Team Members
- Managing delivery and expectations
- Taking action to ensure the success of the project.

Project Partner

The Project Partner supports the Project Leader, complementing the Project Leader's knowledge, skill and experience. Responsibilities are:

- Assisting the Project Leader in 'two man lift' work
- Quality assuring the Project Leader's work
- Deputising for, the Project Leader in day-to-day management of the project
- Anticipating events and acting to ensure the success of the project.

> *It is good practice for a Project Leader to have a Project Partner. The Project Sponsor should make the appointments during Project Inception.*

Customer Domain Manager

The project role of a domain manager implementing at least one deliverable that enables benefit realisation. Responsibilities are:

- Assessing the impact of the project on their domain
- Agreeing the deliverables to be received, the requirements specification and the related quality standards
- Committing specific resources of own domain to the project
- Empowering a Project Team Member to represent their own domain in the project
- Ensuring that their own domain realises benefits from its participation in the project.

Supplier Domain Manager

The project role of a domain manager creating and deploying resources to make at least one deliverable. Responsibilities are:

- Agreeing the deliverables to be created

- Agreeing the development methods, the requirements specification and the related quality standards to be used for their creation

- Committing specific resources of own domain to the project

- Empowering a Project Team Member to represent their own domain in the project

Project Team Member

A person nominated by a domain manager to be responsible for the completion of agreed work within a domain. Detailed responsibilities may include:

- Ensuring the domain uses the agreed development methods and quality standards to create deliverables that meet the agreed specification

- Planning in detail the work of the domain

- Negotiating target dates and resources with the Project Leader

- Ensuring that the domain delivers as promised.

> *Project Team Members are appointed during Detailed Planning. The role carries no responsibilities until then.*

Benefit Owner

A Benefit Owner is a domain manager who accepts responsibility for realising a project benefit, and who:

- Makes a personal commitment to benefit realisation

- Plans the realisation of the benefit

- Negotiates the benefit amount and realisation date

- Acts to realise the benefit.

> *Benefit Owners are identified during Benefit Planning.*

Role Compatibility

The same person can hold some roles on one project but some are incompatible and can't reasonably be held by the same person.

Other role combinations, whilst not incompatible, may be difficult for one person because there may be a conflict of interest.

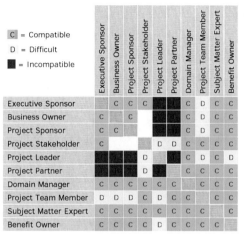

C = Compatible
D = Difficult
■ = Incompatible

	Executive Sponsor	Business Owner	Project Sponsor	Project Stakeholder	Project Leader	Project Partner	Domain Manager	Project Team Member	Subject Matter Expert	Benefit Owner
Executive Sponsor		C	C	C	■	■	C	D	C	C
Business Owner	C		C		■	■	C	D	C	C
Project Sponsor	C	C			■	■	C	D	C	C
Project Stakeholder	C				D	D	C	C	C	C
Project Leader	■	■	D			■	C	D	C	D
Project Partner	■	■	D		■		C	C	C	C
Domain Manager	C	C	C	C	C	C		C	C	C
Project Team Member	D	D	D	C	D	C	C		C	C
Subject Matter Expert	C	C	C	C	C	C	C	C		C
Benefit Owner	C	C	C	C	D	C	C	C	C	

Figure 9: Role Compatibility Chart

What do we start with?

Verdandi's approach to best practice is Value Management. It uses a Bid to set out a simple business case for the idea, which is used to obtain initial funding and form a 'contract' between the Business Owner and Executive Sponsor. Production of a Bid may require the services of a Business Analyst.

Bid

The Bid document has six sections:

- Investment Appraisal – Used to measure the commercial worth against specific investment criteria determined by the organisation
- Initiative Sizing Matrix – Used to assess the complexity (simple, moderate, complex, very complex) and the business risk (minimal, low, high, very high)
- Initiative Scorecard – Used to assess the potential contribution that it will make to the business strategy
- Initiative Details – Describes the work as currently understood; and is the Project Leader's starting point
- Value Analysis – Identifies the sensitivities to establish the chance of higher or lower benefit
- Cost Benefit Analysis - Lists the financial and non-financial benefits, manpower and costs as currently understood within stated margins of error.

A project starts once the Change Board has accepted the Bid and approved initial funding for the idea. At least the Initiative Details and Cost Benefit Analysis are required to start any project.

Initial funding is used to get a project to the point where the feasibility and viability can be confirmed, and sufficient information exists for full funding to be approved or for a decision to be taken to re-scope or terminate the project.

It funds:

- Early business analysis and design
- Project definition and planning
- Essential research and consultancy
- Production of a full Business Case, if required.

For the duration of the project, the Project Leader keeps the Cost Benefit Analysis up-to-date as information is refined and changed through definition and planning.

If at any stage the Cost Benefit Analysis changes beyond the limits of the Business Owner's authority, the Bid has to be re-submitted to the Change Board for re-approval.

Project Inception

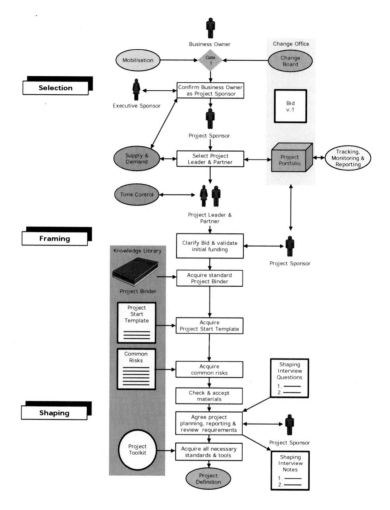

Figure 10: Project Inception Process Map

Project Inception is the process that launches the project successfully, puts in place key role holders, and agrees the project management approach and infrastructure.

> **Many projects fail for no other reason than poor quality inception. Project Inception creates the project's 'terms of engagement' - skimp on this at your peril!**

Project Inception for a project or programme is authorised by the Change Board. If the project is part of a programme, inception will be authorised by the Steering Committee during Mobilisation.

Selection

Steps

R = Responsible
A = Accountable
C = Contribute
I = Informed

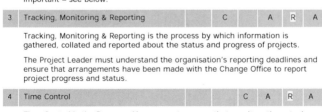

		Executive Sponsor	Head of Demand	Head of Supply	Project Sponsor	Project Leader	Project Partner
1	Confirm Business Owner as Project Sponsor (Gate 1)	R	A	A	A		

The Executive Sponsor is responsible for empowering the Business Owner and confirming them as the Project Sponsor.

| 2 | Select Project Leader & Project Partner | I | A | A | R | C | C |

The Project Sponsor is responsible for the selection and appointment of the Project Leader and Project Partner.

The Head of Supply will identify suitable candidates for interview. During the Project Leader interview process the Project Sponsor will:

- Evidence key competencies and necessary skills

- Probe experience, achievements and project management knowledge

- Satisfy themselves that the candidate is capable of leading the delivery of a successful project.

Areas of exposure are covered by a Project Partner. The Project Partner role is important – see below.

| 3 | Tracking, Monitoring & Reporting | | | C | | A | R | A |

Tracking, Monitoring & Reporting is the process by which information is gathered, collated and reported about the status and progress of projects.

The Project Leader must understand the organisation's reporting deadlines and ensure that arrangements have been made with the Change Office to report project progress and status.

| 4 | Time Control | | | | C | A | R | A |

Time Control is the Resource Management process that monitors the actual against planned use of manpower, person by person to account for resource utilisation and enable invoices from external suppliers and cross-charges from internal suppliers to be verified.

Time Control helps prevent resources being squandered and identifies high and low performers.

The Project Leader must ensure that all necessary arrangements have been made with the Change Office.

When suppliers are working to 'time and materials' contracts, Time Control is essential.

Why have a Project Partner?

> **The Project Partner's role is to anticipate and act to ensure success.**

In most project leadership situations it is unlikely that any one person will have all the skills, experience and knowledge needed for a given project - it is easier to find two people who together have all the necessary attributes.

Two people working in partnership accomplish more than two individuals – with the same incredible effect on difficult or complex work as a 'block and tackle' has on lifting heavy objects – work is moved faster, with significantly less effort and risk.

Some project work is done better by two people working in partnership than by one person working alone. This includes interviewing, planning, facilitating workshops and quality assurance. On projects, this adds up to less errors, ommissions and oversights.

A Project Partner is used to lessen reliance on the Project Leader and open up the opportunity to develop new talent within the organisation. A Project Partner can also provide:

- Challenges to the Project Leader's thinking
- Subject matter expertise
- Coaching and mentoring support for problem solving
- Continuity in cases of unavoidable absence
- Contacts and additional relationships.

Typically, the Project Leader provides about 90% of the project leadership effort and the Project Partner about 10%.

When capabilities are traded across an organisation, using Project Leaders to partner each other, nothing is added to the overall cost of project leadership.

In short, there is no increase in cost or the amount of work. The work gets completed more effectively and to a higher quality so greatly increasing the probability of success.

Selection Checklist

1	Does your Project Sponsor understand the responsibilities of the role?
2	Is your Project Sponsor prepared to devote the time and energy to discharge the responsibilities of the role?
3	Do you know the tracking, monitoring and reporting requirements of the Change Office?
4	Do you and your Project Partner between you have the necessary knowledge, key competencies, skills, and experience?
5	Has your Project Sponsor empowered you to deliver the project?
6	Has the project portfolio been updated to show your and your Project Partner's appointments?
7	Have you established a Time Control process with the Change Office?

Throughout this guide if your answer to any Selection Checklist question is 'no', then seek advice and guidance, take the appropriate action or raise it as an issue.

Framing

Steps

		Executive Sponsor	Head of Change	Head of Supply	Project Sponsor	Project Leader	Project Partner
	R = Responsible						
	A = Accountable						
	C = Contribute						
	I = Informed						
1	Clarify Bid and validate initial funding	I	A		A	R	A

The Project Leader is responsible for ensuring that the Bid is complete, unambiguous, and error free. It is inevitable that there will be some aspects that the Project Leader and Project Partner find confusing; these should be clarified by questioning of the Project Sponsor.

It is also possible that, from their knowledge and experience, the Project Leader and Project Partner will spot omissions and oversights. These should be clarified in discussion with the Project Sponsor.

Common causes of project failure include:

- Projects not aligning with the organisation's strategic imperatives

- Business cases driven by initial price and not looking at whole-life value taking account of capital, maintenance, and service costs

- Not assessing the chance of higher or lower benefits.

Review the completeness of the business case and the adequacy of initial funding. If any aspects are in doubt, appropriate changes to the Bid should be agreed with the Project Sponsor, Executive Sponsor and Head of Change.

2	Acquire standard Project Binder				C	I	R	I

The Project Leader is responsible for project documentation.

Project Documentation will be largely electronic. However, the Project Leader should keep the current version of all key documents in a standard Project Binder both for quick reference and as an aid to discussions.

3	Acquire Project Start Template				C	R	I

The Project Start Template is a standard list of all the recommended tasks and activities that a Project Leader should consider in defining, planning, delivering, reviewing and closing a project in Task & Activity List format.

4	Acquire common risks				C	R	I

Within the Knowledge Library will be lists of risks common to all and particular project types. Using the common risks as a guide, determine if similar sensitivities exist within the project, and incorporate relevant risks into the Risk Log.

5	Check & accept materials				A	R	A

A project incepted on the basis of a weak Bid is doomed to failure. The Project Sponsor is perfectly entitled to ask for the Project Leader and Project Partner to confirm its adequacy from a project delivery perspective.

Framing Checklist

1	Do you and your Project Partner fully understand the Bid?
2	Have all omissions and oversights been clarified with the Project Sponsor?
3	Have you incorporated the relevant common risks into the Risk Log?
4	Is the initial funding adequate?
5	Have you acquired and set up your standard Project Binder?
6	Have you acquired your Project Start Template?

Shaping

Steps

		Executive Sponsor	Head of Demand	Head of Supply	Project Sponsor	Project Leader	Project Partner
	R = Responsible						
	A = Accountable						
	C = Contribute						
	I = Informed						
1	Agree project planning, reporting & review requirements				A	R	A

The Project Leader is responsible for agreeing the project shape with the Project Sponsor. The discussion need take no more than one hour and is best led by the Project Leader with the Project Partner taking notes. The Project Leader should use standard shaping interview questions and prepare for the meeting.

The Project Leader should record the project shape using the Shaping Interview Notes and send them to the Project Sponsor for sign-off.

2	Acquire all necessary standards & tools				C	R	A

Appropriate planning and reporting tools should be selected according to the size and nature of the project – see Project Toolkit™.

All tools should be maintained under version control – see Techniques.

Project Shape

The project shape is the Project Sponsor's view of how the project will be run:

1   Who is the Executive Sponsor?

2   Who are the Project Stakeholders?

> **Stakeholders are people, teams and domains that have the power to influence the outcome of a project. They may include audiences internal and external to the organisation.**

- If a stakeholder is a group of people, for example, the external customer, select a person in the organisation to represent the 'voice of' the external customer and appoint them as a Project Stakeholder

- The Project Sponsor should invite people to accept the role of Project Stakeholder - the names can then be confirmed.

3   What is the preferred approach to planning? The options are:

- Planning to the end, in detail, based on documented assumptions; this is the option most likely to result in project success; planning in detail is not expensive and it establishes the ability to control project activity within domains where there is no direct authority

- Planning, and delivering, in stages - planning in stages does not alert the organisation to the total manpower, costs and time-scales

- Planning only at high level - this is a relatively high-risk option and is only likely to result in success if the project is simple or the suppliers are very competent and reliable.

4   Given your experience of the delivery track record of the internal and external suppliers involved in the project, to what level of detail do you want their activities planned and controlled?

- Suppliers who have an excellent track record may be lightly managed, focusing on the Deliverable Log rather than the Task & Activity List.

- Suppliers who have no track record, or whose track record is poor, are best 'close-managed' with control exercised through the Task & Activity List – see Detailed Planning.

5   Is there a Target Operating Model to which we must conform?

6   What reporting do you require, at what frequency and to whom should reports be circulated? The choice is between the summary Progress Report and individual reports. The first three are always recommended:

- Milestone Report

- Issue List

- Risk Log

- Key Deliverable Report

- Cost Control

- Manpower Control

- Change Log

- Critical Success Factor Log

- Benefit Report.

7   How will unresolved issues threatening a milestone be reported to the Executive Sponsor by the Project Leader? The Issue List is recommended.

> The **Issue List** is the Project Leader's defence against intransigence and ineffectuality – see Issue Management.

8   What is the scale of the required Communication Plan?

> A **Communication Plan** should be considered as a deliverable of every project – see Communication Management.

9   What project reviews do you require and at what frequency?

> A review is an examination of the conduct and performance of a project, at any time, in relation to the organisation's project management processes and quality standards.

10   Is the project subject to audit or inspection?

> An audit is an examination of the project's probity. An inspection is an unscheduled examination of the compliance of a project in relation to regulatory or legal requirements, industry standards or the organisation's quality standards.

11   Is a Steering Committee needed?

> **A Steering Committee is more appropriate to a programme than a project.**

A Steering Committee is not normally needed for a project. Meetings between the Project Sponsor and Project Leader, and sometimes Project Stakeholders usually suffice. See Using a Steering Committee.

12   Who is responsible for authorising expenditure and what is the process?

13   Who is responsible for sanctioning a change request? This is normally the Project Sponsor. Under what criteria would the Change Board consider de-committing from the project?

Shaping Checklist

1	Are all aspects of the project shape reasonable, practical, and agreed?
2	Do you have electronic copies of all planning and control tools?
3	Has the project shape been agreed with the Project Sponsor?
4	Are you empowered to escalate issues?

Tips

- Having a Project Partner is a sign of strength not a sign of weakness
- The most effective Project Leader and Project Partner combination is where each person views a situation from a different perspective - expect and welcome 'constructive tension' - if two people think the same, do the same and behave the same - one is unnecessary
- Take time to agree how you will work together with your Project Partner, paying particular attention to each other's strengths and responsibilities
- The Bid is almost certain to contain ambiguities and omissions, have oversights and relatively large margins of error – assume nothing: ask for clarification from the Project Sponsor and take advice from relevant subject matter experts
- Ensure that the initial funding is adequate before proceeding
- Do not skimp on any aspect of Project Inception.

Project Definition

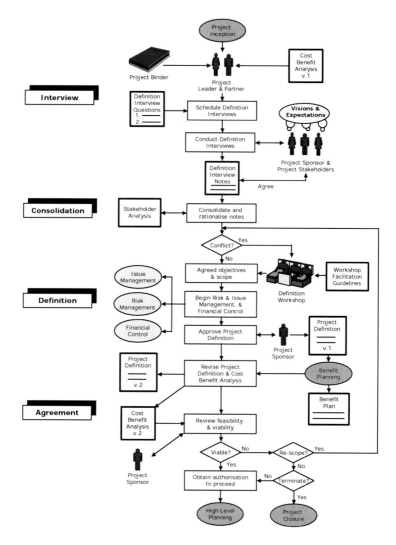

Figure 11: Project Definition Process Map

Project Definition ideally follows the completion of Project Inception but can begin as soon as the Project Sponsor has identified the Project Stakeholders. Project Definition:

- Establishes a common, balanced and agreed view of what has to be done and by when
- Identifies the project objectives and scope, key deliverables and expectations.

> The **Project Definition** is the 'contract' between the **Project Sponsor** and the **Project Leader**. It sets the criteria by which project success will be assessed.

The Project Definition and the Cost Benefit Analysis form the starting point for the Benefit Planning process, after which, it is likely that both will need revision.

Interview

Steps

		Project Sponsor	Project Stakeholder	Project Leader	Project Partner	Head of Chnage
R = Responsible						
A = Accountable						
C = Contribute						
I = Informed						
1	Schedule Definition Interviews	A	A	R	A	

Definition Interview Questions are applicable to all projects. The aim of the interview is to record the interviewee's personal perception of the project, which is used to prepare the Project Definition.

Each interview is with one interviewee – the Project Sponsor or a Project Stakeholder - and should be booked for one hour. It's good practice to send the interview questions to each interviewee in advance.

2	Conduct Definition Interviews	A	A	R	A	

Prior to an interview, the Project Leader and Project Partner should prepare for successful interview – see Techniques. The interview is best held face-to-face – although a videoconference or teleconference is acceptable.

Avoid having the 'interviewee' answer the questions by email – discussion adds considerable clarity and insight. It is best if the notes taken at the interview are the words spoken by the interviewee. Any paraphrasing should be validated by the 'note-taker' with the interviewee during the interview.

3	Validate Interview Notes	A	A	R	A	

Interview notes should be written up as soon as possible after the interview using the Definition Interview Notes tool. The Project Leader should send these notes to the interviewee for amendment and confirmation that 'they are an accurate and complete record' – approved interview notes are valuable should a dispute arise later.

Definition Interview Questions

1   *At which strategic imperatives is the project aimed?*

    The responses are raw material for the Background
    section of the Project Definition and will confirm the
    Initiative Scorecard entries in the Bid.

2   *What is your vision of the improvements that the project
    will bring about?*

    The responses will help validate the objectives, scope
    and key deliverables sections of the Project Definition.

3   *What do you see as being the objectives of the project?*

    An objective is a targeted achievement of the project
    aimed at the initiative purpose and against which it will
    be measured. Each objective needs to be 'SMART' -
    Specific; Measurable; Achievable; Relevant; Time
    bound.

4   *In meeting the objectives, what factors do you see as
    being critical to success?*

    A critical success factor is a significant entity to which
    achievement of objectives and realisation of benefits is
    critical, and which must be within limits in order to
    achieve success.

5   *What entities (things) do you see as being included in
    and excluded from the scope of the project?*

    The boundaries, dimensions and interfaces of the
    initiative clearly define what is included, and what is
    excluded from the scope of the project.

6   *What do you see as the key deliverables of the project?*

    A deliverable is any change, enabler or component of
    change, which contributes to the achievement of at least
    one objective, and hence the realisation of benefit, and
    which must be formally approved or accepted.

    A key deliverable is a deliverable that is pivotal and for
    which progress towards a deadline is to be reported -
    when complete, it enables the realisation of specific
    benefit.

7   *What important deadlines must be achieved?*

    A deadline is a date, in this context for the completion of
    a key deliverable, that if not achieved will cause the
    project to fail.

8   *What are the important quality standards to which we
    must adhere?*

    A quality standard is a specific parameters or definition
    by which the quality of a deliverable can be assessed:

- For compliance with statutory, regulatory, legal, or industry standards
- To mitigate risk
- To attain accreditation.

9   *What working environment considerations could impact project success in either a positive or restrictive way?*

These considerations may refer to markets, geography, culture, policy, working practices and development methods. The responses are raw material for the constraints section of the Project Definition.

10   *What interdependencies on actions or with other initiatives exist?*

An interdependency is a relationship which determines that:

- An event cannot start until an event in another initiative has been completed
- Two or more events each in different initiatives must start and/or end together.

The responses are raw material for the constraints section of the Project Definition.

11   *What constraints will affect the project?*

A constraint is a physical, financial, or time limitation or boundary within which the project must proceed – staying within a constraint is not optional!

12   *What assumptions are being made in carrying out the project?*

An assumption is a statement of supposed fact accepted as true for the purposes of planning, which should be assessed for risk and opportunity and replaced by a clear decision by the end of planning or, if refuted, converted to an issue.

13   *What do you see as the key areas of cost and benefit?*

The responses may be used to validate the Cost Benefit Analysis.

14   *What do you see as the major sensitivities and associated risks?*

A sensitivity is a factor to which the outcome of an event is sensitive. It may be controllable, in which case the work to control it must be in the project plan or uncontrollable in which case it is the source of risk to delivery or the chance of lower benefit.

Sensitivities may be used as a starting point in the creation of the Risk Log and are raw material for the critical success factor section of the Project Definition.

15   *Is there anything that might block progress or inhibit success?*

These should be formulated as issues.

16   *What situations would cause you to review whether to proceed further with the project or alter its direction?*

The responses are raw material for the constraints section of the Project Definition.

17   *Is there any other information of which we should be aware?*

Interview Checklist

1	Have the definition interviews been scheduled? Are the arrangements – face-to-face, videoconference and teleconference – satisfactory?
2	Does the Project Leader have a partner for each interview to make notes of the interviewee's responses?
3	Has adequate time been allowed for preparation, 'write-up', validation by the interviewee and amendment?
4	Have the interviewees been given the opportunity to validate their interview notes – and has each given a 'sign-off'?

Consolidation

Steps

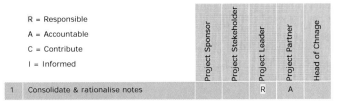

		Project Sponsor	Project Stakeholder	Project Leader	Project Partner	Head of Chnage
1	Consolidate & rationalise notes			R	A	

The responses are best collated on one Definition Interview Notes tool. Any duplicate responses can be then easily removed.

Any responses that are conflicting should be highlighted for resolution. The extent and nature of commitment can be assessed using the Stakeholder Analysis tool.

2	Conflict?	R	A	A	C	

If conflicting responses exist, it will not be possible to create a Project Definition supported by all Project Stakeholders.

The Project Leader should meet with the Project Sponsor to discuss possible solutions to the conflict. It may be possible to resolve some of the differences by the Project Sponsor having a one-to-one discussion with a Stakeholder. However, where major differences exist, a Definition Workshop will be required.

3	Agreed Objectives & Scope	A	A	R	A	

Before creating the Project Definition, it is wise to check that all Project Stakeholders and the Project Sponsor are committed to the objectives and scope.

R = Responsible
A = Accountable
C = Contribute
I = Informed

Definition Workshop

A Definition Workshop is a facilitated meeting between the Project Sponsor and the Project Stakeholders with a purpose to resolve inconsistencies and ambiguities, and unanimously agrees the objectives and scope of the project.

The Project Leader will most likely facilitate the event with the Project Partner co-facilitating and Project Sponsor holding the Chair. See – Workshop Facilitation Guidelines.

Stakeholder Management

Management of stakeholder commitment and expectations continues throughout the project and is the responsibility of the Project Sponsor, supported by the Project Leader.

The Project Leader and Project Partner should assess the perceived level of commitment of each stakeholder and identify the perceived resistance, and the changes that might be needed.

Stakeholder Analysis

> **Stakeholder Analysis** *is a tool used to evaluate the commitment of people who have the power to influence the outcome of a project to the changes that might be needed.*

A view can be taken of each stakeholder's actual and required level of commitment:

- Make it happen
- Help it happen
- Advocate
- Indifferent
- Unconvinced
- Uncooperative
- Hostile

If a stakeholder is displaying a lower or higher than required level of commitment, the perceived resistance can generally be determined by tactful discussion.

This will mean understanding the Project Stakeholder's own view of the needs or their personal objectives and why the project objectives and scope might conflict. Once the reason for the resistance is understood, the Project Sponsor and Project Leader can agree the appropriate action to gain commitment. This will mean either altering the project's objectives or persuading the Project Stakeholder to think and behave differently.

The Communication Plan can be used to influence stakeholders, domain managers and other audiences.

Consolidation Checklist

1	Have all the responses in the Definition Interview Notes been combined?
2	Have all conflicting responses been highlighted?
3	Has the need or otherwise for a Definition Workshop been agreed?
4	Has the Definition Workshop, if required, been scheduled with Project Sponsor and Project Stakeholders, and a facilitator and co-facilitator appointed?
5	Are the objectives and scope of the project agreed by the Project Sponsor and all the Project Stakeholders?
6	Has a Stakeholder Analysis been completed and all appropriate expectation management actions delegated?

Definition

Steps

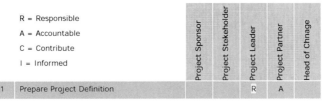

R = Responsible
A = Accountable
C = Contribute
I = Informed

		Project Sponsor	Project Stakeholder	Project Leader	Project Partner	Head of Chnage
1	Prepare Project Definition			R	A	

The Project Leader drafts the Project Definition document from the consolidated interview notes.

The Project Partner should quality assure the draft against the Quality Assurance Criteria below, and the Project Leader make corrections. The cycle should be repeated until the Project Partner is satisfied – expect at least three such iterations.

| 2 | Begin Financial Control | I | | R | A | |

Using the Cost Benefit Analysis and the relevant responses of the Project Sponsor and Project Stakeholders the Project Leader should create the first version of the Cost Estimate.

It may not be possible at this stage to identify the 'owner' of each item of cost, determine appropriate cost codes or establish when the expenditure will be incurred.

| 3 | Begin Risk Management | I | | R | A | |

All known risks including relevant, common risks should be entered in the Risk Log.

It will not be possible at this stage to completely identify and evaluate all risks to an acceptable level of confidence or plan appropriate mitigating actions and contingency plans.

| 4 | Begin Issue Management | I | I | R | A | I |

Issues will occur from the very outset of the project. If the Issue Log has not been created before, the Project Leader should start it now. The first edition of the Issue List should also be circulated.

| 5 | Approve Project Definition | R | I | A | A | I |

The Project Sponsor must approve and sign-off the Project Definition. This will be version 1.0. A copy of the Project Definition should be sent to any appropriate stakeholder.

| 6 | Benefit Planning | R | A | C | C | A |

The Project Sponsor is responsible for Benefit Planning, which starts from the Cost Benefit Analysis and the approved version of the Project Definition. There is an onus on the Project Leader to ensure that Benefit Planning is adequately carried out – see Benefit Planning.

| 7 | Revise Project Definition & Cost Benefit Analysis | R | I | A | A | I |

The Cost Benefit Analysis and Project Definition used to start Benefit Planning will almost certainly need revision. Project Sponsor approval of the revised version is required.

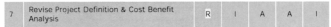

Project Definition

The Project Definition is the 'contract' between the Project Leader and the Project Sponsor for the delivery of the project.

Background

The background is a short narrative statement outlining the origins of the project, why it is being undertaken and its purpose, and value in relation to identified business needs or strategic imperatives.

It comes from the Initiative Details section of the Bid and is consolidated from the responses of the Project Sponsor and Project Stakeholders to the Definition Interview Questions.

Objectives

Each objective is a targeted achievement of the project aimed at the initiative purpose and against which it will be measured.

Each objective needs to 'SMART' - Specific; Measurable; Achievable; Relevant; Time bound. An objective needs to be precise and concise.

They are formed from the consolidated responses of the Project Sponsor and Project Stakeholders to the Definition Interview Questions.

Critical Success Factors

Each critical success factor is a significant entity to which achievement of objectives and realisation of benefits is critical, and which must be within limits in order to achieve success.

Critical success factors are first considered in the Value Analysis section of the Bid, added to from the responses of the Project Sponsor and Project Stakeholders to the Definition Interview Questions and re-considered during Risk Management.

A Critical Success Factor Log may aid control and reporting.

Scope

The scope of the project is the boundaries, dimensions and interfaces of the initiative that clearly identify what is included, and what is excluded. The scope should be precise, concise, unambiguous and comprehensive.

In-scope and out-of-scope entities are listed separately and are formed from the responses of the Project Sponsor and Project Stakeholders to the Definition Interview Questions.

Assumptions

Each assumption is a statement of supposed fact accepted as true for the purposes of planning, which should be assessed for risk and opportunity or replaced by a clear decision by the end of planning or if refuted converted to an issue.

They come from the Initiative Details section of the Bid and are consolidated with the responses of the Project Sponsor and Project Stakeholders to the definition interview questions.

If there are many assumptions, an Assumption Log may aid control.

Constraints

Each constraint is a physical, financial, or time limitation or boundary within which the project must proceed.

They come from the Initiative Details section of the Bid and are consolidated with the responses of the Project Sponsor and Project Stakeholders to the Definition Interview Questions.

Care should be taken that each constraint is a real boundary or limitation rather than one which is imagined.

Key Deliverables

A deliverable is any change, enabler or component of change, which contributes to the achievement of at least one objective, and hence the realisation of benefit, and which must be formally approved or accepted.

Each key deliverable is a deliverable that is pivotal and for which progress towards a deadline is to be reported - when complete, it enables the realisation of specific benefit.

The 'final owner' will be the manager of the domain that is responsible for its 'sign-off'.

Key deliverables come from the Initiative Details section of the Bid and are consolidated with the responses of the Project Sponsor and Project Stakeholders to the Definition Interview Questions.

Approach & Estimated Effort

The approach is a complete but concise description of the project work to be carried out. It sets out an initial structured view of the phases and stages of the project in a logical and chronological sequence within a numbered structure, giving a clear indication of the approach that will be used to create the key deliverables.

If the project is being undertaken for or with another organisation, and is dependent upon that organisation completing certain work in order for the project to advance, then 'our responsibilities' and 'your responsibilities' should be separately identified.

Estimated effort defines the number of standard man-days required for completion of the project work and the project management.

Note: Effort should only be estimated in the Project Definition if the work involved is fully understood. This is to avoid setting expectations that cannot be realised.

In these instances:

- State if the total estimated effort includes the manpower from all domains impacted. If not, state the domains that have been excluded. If appropriate, show manpower from different domains in distinct columns

- Effort required for project management should be shown as a distinct item and should include the effort required for both planning and control. As a guideline, the effort required for project management should not differ significantly from 15% of the total estimated effort for the whole project

- A contingency allowance is shown as a distinct item, expressed as a percentage of the total estimated effort. Contingency is calculated in relation to your perception of the exposure to delivery risk, as you judge it at this stage. Guidelines are:

Exposure to delivery risk	Suggested Contingency Allowance
Minimal	Nil
Low	10%
Moderate	25%
High	40%
Very high	>40%

Following High Level Planning and Detailed Planning, risks will be made apparent and manpower contingency can be adjusted.

Estimated effort should be described as: 'the best estimate at this point, a firm estimate will be provided following Detailed Planning'.

The Project Leader develops their approach from an understanding of the project, supplemented by advice from subject matter experts.

The project work effort, at this stage, is the manpower identified in the Cost Benefit Analysis.

Approach & Estimated Effort

No	Description	Man-days	
1	Project work phase 'A'		
2	Project work phase 'B'		
3	Project work phase 'C'		
Etc	Etc		
	Total		
	Project Management		15%
	Contingency		10%
	Final Total		

Contacts

Lists the names of the people who will be undertaking specific roles in the project. The list, at this stage, should include:

- Project Sponsor
- Project Stakeholders
- Project Leader
- Project Partner
- Domain managers.

It is unlikely that all supplier domains will have been identified at this stage.

Authorisation

Signed by the Project Sponsor on behalf of all the Project Stakeholders and by the Project Leader. Denotes that the Project Definition is accurate, the success criteria are acceptable and the project may proceed to High Level Planning.

Quality Assurance Criteria

A fit-for-purpose Project Definition will:

- Be written in plain business English
- Describe the background adequately but briefly, and clearly identify the business needs
- Define SMART objectives that are precise, concise and aimed at the initiative purpose?
- State all known critical success factors
- State clearly what is included and what is excluded in the project scope
- Adequately cover any exposure with clear assumptions and constraints
- Identify all key deliverables with associated deadlines
- Have a clear and defensible approach effort estimate
- List all known contacts and state their roles
- Be signed-off by the Project Sponsor.

Definition Checklist

1	Is the Project Definition to be submitted fit-for-purpose?
2	Has the first edition of the Risk Log been created?
3	Has the first edition of the Issue Log been created and the first edition of the Issue List circulated?
4	Has the Project Sponsor approved the Project Definition?

Agreement

Steps

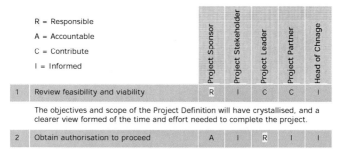

		Project Sponsor	Project Stekeholder	Project Leader	Project Partner	Head of Chnage
	R = Responsible A = Accountable C = Contribute I = Informed					
1	Review feasibility and viability	R	I	C	C	I

The objectives and scope of the Project Definition will have crystallised, and a clearer view formed of the time and effort needed to complete the project.

2	Obtain authorisation to proceed	A	I	R	I	I

If the project is considered feasible, achievable and viable, the Project Sponsor should authorise the Project Leader to proceed to High Level Planning.

Tips

- Don't skimp on the project definition process – if you do, it will reduce the likelihood of success

- If it's simple, it won't take long to write down - if it isn't simple, you need to write it down

- It's always the Project Leader who has misunderstood, never the Project Sponsor

- Be careful not to confuse specification with definition

- Recommend a Definition Workshop to resolve conflicting views

- Never proceed with a project unless the Project Definition document:

  - Is unambiguous, precise and concise

  - Shows that the project is achievable, viable and aimed at identified business needs

  - Has the unified commitment of the Project Sponsor and Project Stakeholders

- If the project involves many customer domains, press for a Benefit Workshop – see Benefit Planning

- Terminating a project is a sign of strength, not a sign of weakness.

High Level Planning

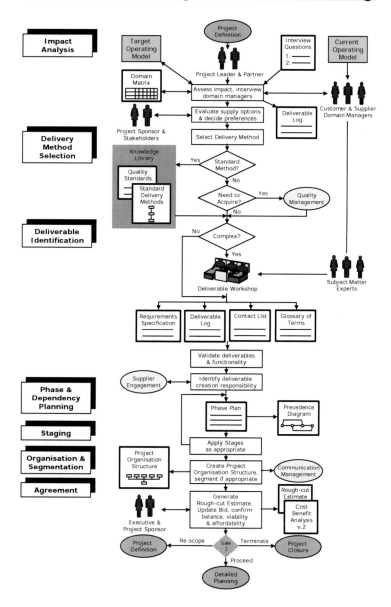

Figure 12: High Level Planning Process Map

High Level Planning ideally follows the completion of the Project Definition process but can begin as soon as the Project Sponsor has approved the Project Definition document. High Level Planning is the process that:

- Establishes the development methods, deliverables, specifications, quality standards and dependencies within a project
- Shows in outline how the project will be conducted and achieved
- Creates a revised Cost Benefit Analysis for the project.

The current Cost Benefit Analysis, the Project Definition and the Benefit Plan form the starting point for High Level Planning.

Impact Analysis

Impact Analysis is the assessment of the potential impact of a project on the current internal and external domains, assets, and future capabilities of the organisation by reference to its current operating model and, if applicable, the Target Operating Model.

Steps

		Project Sponsor	Project Stakeholder	Project Leader	Domain Manager	Design Authority
R = Responsible						
A = Accountable						
C = Contribute						
I = Informed						
1	Assess impact on current operating model	I		R	A	

Impacts on the current operating model are determined by interviewing customer and supplier domain managers, using the questions below.

> *A supplier domain deploys resources to create at least one deliverable, whereas a customer domain implements at least one deliverable to enable planned benefit realisation.*

Interviews should be carried out in a similar way to the definition interviews – the Project Leader and Project Partner form an interviewing team. Findings are recorded in the Domain Matrix.

The Domain Matrix is a tool used to record the analysis of impact of the project on the on the current internal and external domains and assets of the organisation. It identifies each domain as a customer or supplier, names the manager and gives an initial qualitative description of the expected impact.

To ensure the project is driven by business needs, the Project Leader should commence by interviewing customer domain managers, followed by supplier domain managers.

Care should be taken to identify all impacted domains when completing the Domain Matrix. It is almost certain that all the main customer domains will be known at this stage.

Domains can be 'nested' with several smaller domains within a larger domain. Lower level customer domains can be identified later.

Some external supplier domains will not yet be known because either there are several possible suppliers and a final selection is still to be made or no possible supplier of the required delivered has yet been identified. In either case, it is best to record a notional supplier domain in the Domain Matrix.

If the project needs to engage external suppliers then refer to the Supplier Engagement process and work in close consultation with the organisation's procurement function.

2	Assess Target Operating Model impact	I	-	R	A	I

Many organisations have a Target Operating Model in some form, maintained by a Business Architect and a Technical Architect, under the direction of a Design Authority. A Target Operating Model typically illustrates the business and technical capabilities of an organisation in seven 'layers'. It is used in a business in a similar way that an architect's design blueprint is used in the construction of a building.

The Project Leader needs expert guidance in order to assess the impact of the project on the future capabilities and confirm that this is within the scope of the model. If the impacts are compatible, all is well. If not, the Project Sponsor should be informed and the Project Leader needs to identify the incompatibility and escalate the issues to the Design Authority.

3	Create Deliverable Log		I		R	A	

If the Project Leader has not already done so, now is the time to create the first version of the Deliverable Log. The starting point for the Deliverable Log is the key deliverables from the Project Definition, supplemented by any other deliverables so far identified.

4	Evaluate options & decide preferences	A	A	R	C	I

There are sometimes different ways of achieving a required outcome. For example, should you build something or buy a ready-made solution?

It's much easier to make a decision after the requirements have been specified and agreed, and the costs and sensitivities of each option are known. However, this may not be until later in the project.

Early decisions taken to rule out infeasible options using subjective evaluation will reduce the time and effort needed to specify, and plan the project. The Project Leader should work with the Project Sponsor and Project Stakeholders to evaluate options based on what is known or what can easily be found out. Most often, one option will stand out head and shoulders above all others.

Where there are options for supplying solutions:

- Identify the options

- State, for each option, the advantages, disadvantages, cost considerations and sensitivities

- If one stands out above all others, rule out those which are infeasible and plan the project, and build the Cost Benefit Analysis around the preferred option

- Otherwise plan for the preferred option to be decided after the requirements have been specified.

Where certain options cannot be ruled out because the differences are not obvious, it will be necessary to make the decision after the analysis and design has taken place and the precise requirements have been specified.

Domain Manager Questions

> *The Project Leader should describe the project bearing in mind confidentiality. Consider using a non-disclosure agreement, if appropriate.*

Customer Domain

1. Have you been made aware of this project?

2. What are the specific project deliverables that would bring benefit to your domain?

> *A deliverable is a change which contributes towards at least one objective, and hence the realisation of benefit, created by one domain and formally accepted by another.*

3. What do you need to change in your domain to accommodate the project deliverables?

4. What quality standards should apply and do they exist?

5. What do you see as the costs and benefits?

6. What sensitivities do you foresee and what can we do to avoid the risks and make this project deliver the anticipated benefits?

7. Who, from your domain, can provide relevant subject matter expertise?

8. Is there anyone else that we need to talk to?

Supplier Domain

1. Which development method will you use?

2. What deliverables do you expect to supply?

3. What quality standards need to be applied and do they exist?

4. How would you control and assure the quality of the deliverables you supply?

5. What sensitivities do you foresee and what can we do to avoid the risks and make this project deliver the anticipated benefits?

6. Are there any areas of cost or benefit you think we may have overlooked?

7. Who can provide relevant subject matter expertise?

8. Is there anyone else that we need to talk to?

Third-party Domain

> *It is not unusual for domains to exist that whilst not customers or suppliers, are impacted by the project - these domains should not be ignored.*

Have you been made aware of the project and what can we do to avoid costs and risks, and realise benefits for you?

Deliverable Log

> *The **Deliverable Log** is the definitive record of all the deliverables that will be produced by a project, with key deliverables flagged for reporting purposes.*

The Deliverable Log records each deliverable noting:

- Identifier & description– a three-tier number is used to indicate where deliverables are components of higher-level deliverables

- Version No. – if more than one version of the deliverable needs to be created and tested before it can finally be handed over to the customer, see Version Control

- MoSCoW – the Project Sponsor's indication of necessity

> *It's often possible to de-scope and reduce the cost of a complex key deliverable without compromising quality or benefits by applying 'MoSCoW Analysis' to the **Deliverable Log** and the corresponding **Requirements Specification**:*
>
> - *Must have – to enable realisation of benefit*
>
> - *Should have – to reduce risk to benefit realisation*
>
> - *Could have – if budget is sufficient*
>
> - *Would like – Project Sponsor's options for overcoming objections.*

- Completion deadline – only relevant to key deliverables

- Project Stage / Phase – the phase and, if appropriate, stage in which the deliverable will be delivered

- Creation responsibility

- Planned iterations

> *Iteration is a single cycle of work and quality assurance aimed at the creation of a deliverable.*

- Applicable quality standards

> *A quality standard defines the specific parameters or definitions by which the quality of a deliverable can be assessed:*
>
> - *For compliance with statutory, regulatory, legal, or industry standards*
>
> - *To mitigate risk*
>
> - *To attain accreditation.*

- Domain sign-off – the names of the domains that will approve the deliverable as complete

- Sign-off method – one person or a workshop

- Final owner – the person in business-as-usual responsible for the deliverable after handover

- Complete, De-scoped – indicates if the deliverable has been handed over (C) to the final owner or was de-scoped (D).

Impact Analysis Checklist

1	Have all necessary domain manager interviews taken place and are the interview notes 'signed-off'?
2	Is the Domain Matrix adequate at this stage?
3	Is the impact of the project compatible with the Target Operating Model?
4	If the impact of the project is not compatible, has the Project Sponsor discussed the conflict with the Design Authority?
5	If more than one supply option is applicable, have the options been evaluated and the preferred option chosen?
6	If new external suppliers are involved, have you consulted with procurement to agree the supplier selection process?
7	Has the first version of the Deliverable Log been created?

Development Method Selection

A good development method embodies all the lessons learned by people through practical experience. It is re-used, time-and-again to:

- Save time, effort and money
- Reduce the risk of oversights and omissions
- Ensure a quality product.

A development method is used on a project to help plan the best approach and identify the associated deliverables, and quality standards.

Development methods come in many forms. Figure 13 shows the stages that may be involved in the development of a new product involving an IT application but the same principle can be applied to the efficient development of just about any complex deliverable.

Figure 13: Example Development Method Stages

A development method may be a simple, proven step-by-step process at one extreme to a complete, documented methodology at the other.

Whichever it is, expect it to be presented at the highest level as a 'summary on a page'. See Techniques for a full explanation of what 'Working with a Development Method' involves.

Steps

		Project Sponsor	Domain Manager	Project Leader	Project Partner	Head of Chnage
R = Responsible						
A = Accountable						
C = Contribute						
I = Informed						
1	Standard Methods?		C	R	A	

Internal development methods are acquired or created by the organisation over time and should be available from domain managers or from the Knowledge Library. The Project Leader should determine the availability and whether those proposed are appropriate and acceptable.

The Project Leader should also ensure that appropriate quality standards exist for each deliverable, which are acceptable to domain managers and the Project Sponsor.

2	Need to acquire?		C	R	A	

If there is no known development method or appropriate quality standards for a complex deliverable, or those provided are considered unacceptable, then the Project Leader should seek to acquire or develop a suitable version through the organisation's Quality Management process.

Quality Management

Quality Management is the process an organisation uses to validate the adequacy, continually improve and adapt, or acquire new development methods and quality standards where necessary.

Validation

If the adequacy of a proposed development method or quality standard is in doubt, then it should be validated. If inadequate it must be improved or a new version acquired or developed before it is applied. If the organisation doesn't have a function that provides this service, the work should be done as part of the project.

Acquisition

Development methods and quality standards may be acquired from a variety of sources. For example:

- The public domain – internet or published materials

- From consultants, suppliers or industry associations

- Available as a product that can be purchased.

If they are to be acquired, there will be a cost at least in terms of manpower. Sources other than the public domain generally require payment.

Development

If a suitable version cannot be acquired, then it may be necessary to develop one as part of the project - with or without external specialist advice. Development work is time consuming, expensive and risky, and doing this should be avoided unless the project genuinely involves pioneering. Even then, there may be a similar version in existence upon which another can be modelled.

If the project funding is insufficient to pay the cost of necessary validation, acquisition or development, it is an issue that needs escalation.

Selection Checklist

1	Are needed development methods and quality standards available and fit for purpose?
2	Are any 'missing' development methods and quality standards noted?
3	Is there sufficient funding to pay for the improvement of existing development methods and quality standards as necessary?
4	Is there sufficient funding to pay for the acquisition or development of new development methods and quality standards as necessary?

Deliverable Identification

Many deliverables identified will be 'composite' - made up from the creation of several smaller or simpler enabling or component deliverables.

A subject matter expert can often easily identify the enabling or component deliverables. However, a key deliverable may be sufficiently complex to warrant a Deliverable Workshop.

Deliverable Workshop

> *A Deliverable Workshop is a facilitated meeting involving people representing project suppliers and customers that identify the deliverables to be created by the project at a level of detail adequate for further planning.*

A successful Deliverable Workshop needs appropriate attendance; empowered representatives of all relevant supplier and customer domains should be present, especially subject matter experts.

The Project Leader and Project Partner should focus each workshop on one key deliverable. The aim of the workshop is to answer three questions, from each customer and supplier viewpoint:

1   What deliverables are needed to produce this key deliverable, including all the enablers and components?

> *Checking that all the new things needed, all the existing things that must be improved, all the existing things that are no longer required have been identified for the context in which it is to be implemented.*

2   Which supplier is responsible for creating each deliverable and which customer is responsible for accepting each deliverable?

3   If we are to have these deliverables, what materials and tools are needed?

A Deliverable Workshop also provides the opportunity for views on required functionality, usability and acceptability to be captured.

> *When the deliverable is created, quality itself is not a variable but the specification and quality standards often are.*

Requirements Specification

> **A Requirements Specification** is a description of the
> functionality, usability and acceptability that the
> customer expects from the implementation and
> subsequent operation of the deliverable.
>
> • *Functionality is a list of features and designed
>   actions that are necessary for the deliverable to
>   be adequate for purpose*
>
> • *Usability is the customer's perception of the
>   features that make it usable for the purpose it
>   was intended*
>
> • *Acceptability is the customer's feelings towards
>   the features that mean it will be implemented
>   and operated successfully – that it is fit for
>   purpose.*

The requirements for each deliverable should be specified in
a Requirements Specification, either for the deliverable itself
or for a higher-order, complex deliverable - if the deliverable
is simple, the effort required to specify it should be trivial. If
the deliverable is complex, specification is essential.

The functionality of any key deliverable must be such that
the associated benefits can be realised.

Steps

		Project Sponsor	Domain Manager	Project Leader	Project Partner	Subject Matter Expert
R = Responsible						
A = Accountable						
C = Contribute						
I = Informed						
1	Deliverable Workshop		C	R	A	C

In the Deliverable Workshop the Project Leader and Project Partner adopt the
roles of facilitator and co-facilitator.

Workshop attendees should be encouraged to visualise the deliverable and call
out the enabling and component deliverables. Use of an appropriate
development method will improve the quality of this process.

Information should be recorded in either a straight list or a 'spider' diagram. It
is not uncommon for 200-300 deliverables to be identified for a complex
deliverable - and this can be achieved in a very short space of time.

Some things recorded will be deliverables and others will relate to the
specification – all input should be welcomed.

The Project Leader takes the output from the Deliverable Workshop and
includes it in the Deliverable Log and a Requirements Specification as
appropriate. These should be circulated to workshop attendees for agreement.

Creation of a Requirements Specification will cost time and money and
therefore it should be included on the Deliverable Log as a deliverable.

2	Validate deliverables & functionality	R	C	A	C	C

If a Benefit Workshop has previously taken place, it is easy to demonstrate why each component deliverable is necessary. If not, there is a risk that a necessary deliverable might have been missed or one included that does not support a benefit.

It's often possible to de-scope and reduce the cost of a complex key deliverable without compromising quality or realisation of benefit by applying 'MoSCoW Analysis' to the Deliverable Log and corresponding Requirements Specification:

- Must have – to enable realisation of benefit

- Should have – to reduce risk to benefit realisation

- Could have – if budget is sufficient

- Would like – Project Sponsor's options for overcoming objections.

MoSCoW Analysis needs to involve the Project Sponsor to make final decisions.

Also consider if there is opportunity to salvage components from the existing environment as a way of reducing cost and environmental impact.

3	Identify deliverable creation responsibility	I	C	R	A	C

Identify on the Deliverable Log the supplier responsible for the creation of each deliverable and the customer who will be the final owner - state any applicable quality standards, and the delivery deadline if it is a key deliverable.

In consultation with subject matter experts, determine what tools and quantities of materials are needed to produce the deliverable and include this information as separate schedules in the Requirements Specification.

A contract is needed for each external supplier that encompasses the deliverables they will be producing. A service agreement is discretionary for internal suppliers. See Supplier Engagement.

4	Contact List			C	R	A	I

The contacts from the Project Definition, and others involved should be added to the Contact List – ease of communication between people is vital.

5	Glossary of Terms			C	R	I	A

By this time people will have introduced words and phrases that have special meaning within their disciplines. The Project Leader should agree these meanings with the relevant experts, record them in the Glossary of Terms, and make this freely available to anyone involved in any aspect of the project.

If the meaning of a word or phrase is not in the dictionary, it should be defined in the Glossary of Terms. To define a glossary entry, describe what it looks like and state what it is used for or what it does.

Deliverable Identification Checklist

1	Are Deliverable Workshops needed?
2	Have all identified deliverables been recorded in the Deliverable Log in a hierarchical sequence?
3	Does any deliverable need its own Requirements Specification?
4	Has MoSCoW Analysis been performed to reduce cost?
5	Has the creation responsibility and the final owner of each deliverable been identified and added to the Deliverable Log?
6	Has the Supplier Engagement process commenced with each external and internal supplier?
7	Are the project's Contact List and Glossary of Terms fit-for-purpose?

Phase & Dependency Planning

The purpose of Phase & Dependency Planning is to create a structure for the project work that eliminates all but the unavoidable dependencies and balances risk with speed.

Steps

		Project Sponsor	Domain Manager	Project Leader	Project Partner	Head of Chnage
R = Responsible						
A = Accountable						
C = Contribute						
I = Informed						
1	Blend Development Methods	I	C	R	A	

The first step is to align each process step in each development method to the phases first indicated in the Project Definition approach.

It is inevitable that some process steps won't fit – in which case additional phases will be necessary.

> **A phase is a group of tasks. Deliverables are created by the tasks within a phase.**

2	Agree Phase Plan	A	C	R	A	

The phases, when listed in a logical and roughly chronological order, form the Phase Plan. All deliverables need to be accommodated within one Phase Plan.

3	Assign Deliverables to Phases		C	R	A	

Deliverables are assigned to a phases either because there is a natural affinity between the deliverable and the phase or similar skills required. The result of this work is likely to be:

- Some phases to which no deliverables have been assigned – this is an indication that some deliverables are still to be identified in which case return to the Deliverable Identification process.

- Some deliverables do not fit logically into any phase – this is an indication that an extra phase is required.

4	Create Precedence Diagram	C	C	R	A	

The Precedence Diagram is created from the Phase Plan. It is likely that the first draft of a Precedence Diagram will highlight at least one dependency between two phases.

> **A dependency is a relationship, which determines that an event cannot start until another event has been completed or that two or more events must start and/or end together.**

The Project Leader should seek the agreement of the Project Sponsor to the Precedence Diagram.

During the creation of the Precedence Diagram, any assumptions relating to dependencies need to be added to the Project Definition or, if used, the Assumption Log. Risks should be added to the Risk Log.

Precedence Diagram

The Precedence Diagram is a schematic of the project showing the dependencies between its phases. The Precedence Diagram is used to:

- Illustrate the overall approach to the Project Sponsor and show the true dependencies between phases

- Find ways of reducing the elapsed time of Project Delivery by eliminating false dependencies

- Focus the work of Project Team Members on milestone deadlines during Detailed Planning

- Drive the negotiation of delivery promises.

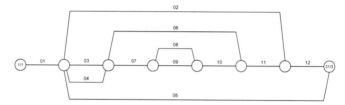

Figure 14: Example Precedence Diagram

Each line represents a phase. Each disc represents a node marking the beginning or end of a phase, which, when dated following detailed planning, becomes a milestone. A milestone is an identified, major point in time when a phase of work within a project must end in order for the project to meet its deadline.

The Precedence Diagram in Figure 14 above shows the project starting on 1st January with a completion deadline of 31st March.

It shows a dependency such that phases 06 and 07 cannot start until phases 03 and 04 are complete. It also shows that the tasks and activities within phase 08 can be carried out at the same time as the tasks and activities within phase 09, and that no dependencies exist between any task or activity within phase 08 and any task or activity within phase 09.

Phase & Dependency Planning Checklist

1	Are all phases and all deliverables now identified, and all deliverables recorded in the Deliverable Log?
2	Is the assignment of deliverables to phases complete?
3	Is the Precedence Diagram logical and optimal, and does it meet with the approval of the Project Sponsor and relevant domain managers?
4	Does the Phase Plan meet with the approval of the Project Sponsor and relevant domain managers?

Staging

> **A stage is a partition of the project at the end of which a decision must be taken to proceed, alter course or terminate.**

Steps

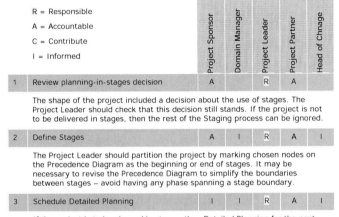

	Project Sponsor	Domain Manager	Project Leader	Project Partner	Head of Chnage
1 Review planning-in-stages decision	A		R	A	

The shape of the project included a decision about the use of stages. The Project Leader should check that this decision still stands. If the project is not to be delivered in stages, then the rest of the Staging process can be ignored.

2 Define Stages	A	I	R	A	I

The Project Leader should partition the project by marking chosen nodes on the Precedence Diagram as the beginning or end of stages. It may be necessary to revise the Precedence Diagram to simplify the boundaries between stages – avoid having any phase spanning a stage boundary.

3 Schedule Detailed Planning	I	I	R	A	I

If the project is to be planned in stages, then Detailed Planning for the next stage should be carried out whilst the preceding stage is being delivered. The elapsed time of a stage is typically about 90 days. Note: Milestones cannot be confirmed until Detailed Planning is complete – unplanned stages will not have dated milestones.

4 Schedule Stage Reviews	A	I	R	A	I

Stage Reviews should be scheduled at milestones.

> **A Stage Review is an assessment of the viability of the project in relation to the success criteria defined in the Project Definition and Cost Benefit Analysis.**

Stage Reviews can be planned but cannot be scheduled until Detailed Planning of the stage is complete.

Stage Review

Typically, the Stage Review report will be presented to the Change Board, which will decide the future of the project.

The de-commit criteria of any supplier contract in a staged project must be geared to the possible review outcomes.

Staging Checklist

1	Has the Project Sponsor confirmed the staging decision made at Project Inception?
2	If the project is to be planned in stages and have all Stage Reviews been scheduled?

Organisation & Segmentation

Steps

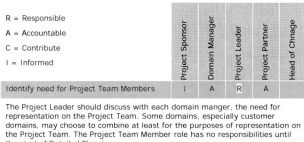

R = Responsible
A = Accountable
C = Contribute
I = Informed

		Project Sponsor	Domain Manager	Project Leader	Project Partner	Head of Chnage
1	Identify need for Project Team Members	I	A	R	A	

The Project Leader should discuss with each domain manger, the need for representation on the Project Team. Some domains, especially customer domains, may choose to combine at least for the purposes of representation on the Project Team. The Project Team Member role has no responsibilities until the start of Detailed Planning.

2	Prepare Project Organisation Structure	I	C	R	A	

The Project Leader will find it helpful to prepare a Project Organisation Structure and make it freely available to all involved in the project.

3	Determine need for segmentation	R	C	A	A	C

It is probably appropriate segment a project into two or more separately managed projects if it:

- Has more than 40 phases of project work

- Requires more than 12 Project Team Members – such a project becomes unwieldy

- Naturally falls into two or more distinct flows of work

Segmented projects may overlap or run in succession, as appropriate.

If the project is segmented into many related families of projects it is better to manage these as a programme, using Programme Management processes to control the overall delivery.

If there are several projects but it does not warrant making it a programme, still consider using a Master Project to co-ordinate the delivery of the projects.

If the Project Leader recommends segmenting a project, the Project Sponsor should discuss the consequences with the Head of Demand. It may be necessary to amend and resubmit the Bid to the Change Board.

4	Communication Plan	R	C	A	A	I

Consider developing your Communication Plan at this point – see Communication Management.

Project Organisation Structure

> The **Project Organisation Structure** depicts the reporting lines between all project roles.

Individuals or teams within customer and supplier domains will carry out the project work. The overall responsibility for this work, and for the implementation of any changes to be made within a domain, is with the domain manager.

The domain manager may combine their role with that of Project Team Member or elect to be represented by a Project Team Member. At the same time, for benefit realisation purposes, each customer domain manager will become a Benefit Owner.

The Project Leader should check that the person has enough time to do the work. The Work Schedule can be used to determine a person's capacity.

Organisation & Segmentation Checklist

1	Has the need for Project Team Members been agreed?
2	Are the Project Organisation Structure, roles and responsibilities, and reporting and escalation paths agreed?
3	Is it appropriate to segment the project?
4	If segmentation is appropriate, has the Project Sponsor agreed relevant actions with the Head of Demand?
5	Have the creation of a Communication Plan been started?

Agreement

Steps

R = Responsible
A = Accountable
C = Contribute
I = Informed

		Project Sponsor	Domain Manager	Project Leader	Project Partner	Head of Chnage
1	Generate Rough-cut Estimate	R		A	A	I

Using the Deliverable Log, roughly estimate the costs, manpower and elapsed time required to create each deliverable. Align the elapsed times to the Precedence Diagram, roughly determine project milestones and 'pencil' these in the nodes. Known costs and manpower can be summed to validate the forecast costs and manpower in the Cost Benefit Analysis.

2	Update Bid	R		A	A	I

Using the documentation created so far – the Project Definition, Benefit Plan, Domain Matrix, Deliverable Log, Precedence Diagram, with 'pencilled in' milestones, Project Organisation Structure and Communication Plan – the Project Leader should review the impact on the Cost Benefit Analysis with the Project Sponsor.

3	Confirm the project balance & review the feasibility and viability (Gate 2)	R		A	A	A

The feasibility and viability of a project will become clearer as it progresses through to the end of detailed planning. It is appropriate to assess feasibility and viability towards the end of High Level Planning.

The Project Leader should present the findings to the Project Sponsor and Executive Sponsor. The decision may be to:

- Approve the project to proceed to Detailed Planning so that the manpower and costs can be accurately determined before asking the Change Board to sanction full funding

- Re-scope the project – in which case it starts again at Project Inception with appropriate initial funding

- Recommend to the Executive Sponsor to terminate and close the project.

Agreement Checklist

1	Are all necessary service agreements and contracts agreed, ready for signature?
2	Have the costs, manpower and elapsed times been roughly estimated from the Deliverable Log?
3	Have milestones been 'pencilled in' the Precedence Diagram?
4	Has the Cost Benefit Analysis been updated?
5	Is the project feasible and viable?
6	Is the project in balance and enough money, manpower and time to complete the agreed work?

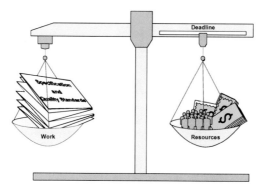

Figure 15: Achieving balance

Tips

- You can usually recover if you get an estimate wrong but it is difficult to recover if you miss out a deliverable
- Use development methods as a means of identifying deliverables and quality standards – avoid suppliers who won't tell you how they intend to do things
- Insist that people explain things in terms you can understand
- Use subject matter experts to help you allocate deliverables to phases and to draw the Precedence Diagram
- If you don't have sufficient knowledge and know-how within the organisation, use external consultancy support
- Use consultants to provide you with the knowledge and know-how - when you have this, reconsider why you might still need them
- Don't expect to get it right first time
- There is always pressure to deliver projects more quickly, less expensively, and using less manpower – don't promise to deliver what cannot be delivered, manage people's expectations
- Discuss the plan with the Project Sponsor. The Project Sponsor will want to be satisfied that the project can deliver:
  - To all deadlines so that the realisation of benefit will proceed as planned
  - Using only the stated resources
  - At a level of risk which is acceptable to the organisation
- Projects will not succeed unless the work, resources and deadline are in balance - be prepared to negotiate and don't try to achieve the impossible
- Consider if a business Continuity Plan might be needed in the event of the project delivering late or failing to deliver at all.

Detailed Planning

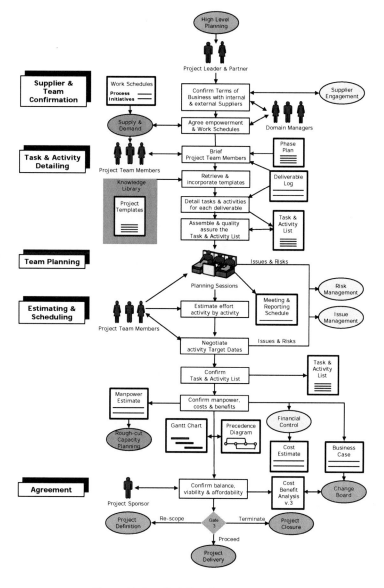

Figure 16: Detailed Planning Process Map

Detailed Planning logically follows High Level Planning. In practice, some aspects – for example, constructing the Task & Activity List – can be carried out alongside High Level Planning.

Detailed Planning is the process that breaks the project down to a level of detail at which:

- Accurate estimates of cost, manpower and time can be made
- The completion of specific activities can be made the responsibility of named Project Team Members
- Risks can be managed
- The Project Leader can be confident in the ability of the project team to deliver successfully.

Project success relies upon meticulous planning and the resolution of skill and resource issues before embarking on Project Delivery.

> *Supplier domains may complain that planning in detail is unnecessary or bureaucratic – the real reason might be that they have insufficient resources or they do not want you to control their activities!*

The Project Leader and Project Team Members may find it beneficial to use software such as MS Project, the 'cut and paste' feature of which enables the Task & Activity List to be constructed at speed.

Supplier & Team Confirmation

Steps

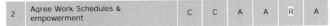

		Project Sponsor	Project Stakeholder	Domain Manager	Project Team Member	Project Leader	Project Partner
R = Responsible A = Accountable C = Contribute I = Informed							
1	Confirm Terms of Business with internal & external suppliers	C	C	A	C	R	A

The Project Leader should confirm that each supplier's Terms of Business are acceptable and that suppliers are at least 'emotionally committed' to delivery, if not committed by formal agreement or contract.

2	Agree Work Schedules & empowerment	C	C	A	A	R	A

The Project Leader should check that each proposed Project Team Member is able to cope, empowered and has the capacity to undertake the work.

People often have a habit of over-committing their own time, which becomes a problem when they need to do work on the project. The available capacity of any role holder to do work can be checked using the Work Schedule.

It takes 10-15 minutes with each Project Team Member to fill out a Work Schedule. It needs to include all current administration, business-as-usual and project-related activity, looking 3 months ahead.

Ask the person to roughly estimate how much effort they need to put into each current activity for them to be successful. This can be entered as hours per day, hours per week or days per month, and converted into days per month and sum this up. Add in the time they will need to put into this project.

It is not uncommon to find that people are already 50% over-committed. If this is the case, when complete the Work Schedule should be taken to the domain manager so that current work can be either triaged or the issue resolved by other means.

Selecting Project Team Members

Each Project Team Member is responsible for the day-to-day control of the project work within a domain and coordinating the transfer of information and material between domains.

A Project Team Member may be the only person doing the project work but is more likely to be leading a team or coordinating the activities of teams and subject matter experts within a domain.

The Project Leader should be confident that each Project Team Member is 'able to cope', that is:

- Where a team is involved, having the proficiency to use influence and interpersonal communication skills
- Having sufficient depth of subject matter understanding of the project work of the domain.

The Project Leader must also ensure that:

- The Project Team Member is empowered by the domain manager – see Empowerment below
- Both the Project Team Member and the domain manager understand the significance of a delivery promise – see Delivery Promise below
- A stand-in is nominated should someone be unavoidably absent - upward delegation is usually preferable.

Empowerment

An empowered Project Team Member is able to take responsibility for the completion of agreed project work to quality, specification, time, and resource targets. To do this requires that the Project Team Member:

- Understands:
  - What work has to be done
  - How it fits in with related work
  - How all that work contributes to the achievement of project objectives.
- Has:

- Skills, knowledge and experience to get the work done

- Human resources to do the work and the financial resources to get it done

- Time to do own work fully and well

- Authority to make all relevant decisions.

If a Project Team Member is not empowered, there is an issue for the domain manager and a related risk to the success of the project.

Delivery Promise

A delivery promise is a negotiated agreement between the promise-giver, typically a Project Team Member, and the promise-taker who is typically the Project Leader. Remember, only empowered people are able to give delivery promises.

The promise is negotiated taking into account:

- The complexity of the work and the skill, and experience of the workers

- The amount of work and the availability of resources

- Any deadlines, natural durations of creative activity, documented assumptions and constraints

- The other work and personal commitments of the co-workers

- Any other factor that the promise-giver can convince the promise-taker is relevant.

A promise is personal and means that work will be completed to the agreed specification and quality standards, by the agreed date, using only the agreed resources, barring unforeseen circumstances. An unexpected circumstance or refuted assumption is no reason to blame the promise-giver. This is an issue for which there is a process.

Supplier & Team Confirmation Checklist

1	Are all suppliers committed to the service agreements, contracts and terms of business that have been agreed?
2	Have all service agreements and contracts been signed?
3	Is each Project Team Member empowered and able to cope?
4	Does each domain manger and Project Team Member understand the significance of a 'delivery promise'?
5	Has the Project Team been formed comprising the Project Leader, the Project Partner and the Project Team Members?
6	Have Project Team Meetings been 'block-booked' in people's diaries?

Task & Activity Detailing

The Task & Activity List is the phases, tasks and activities of a project set out to show in detail:

- How the project will be managed – the Project Leader can write this from a standard Project Start Template

- How each deliverable will be created – determined by Project Team Members and subject matter experts, and assembled by the Project Leader.

> *A task is a set of closely related activities that specifies a distinct piece of work within a phase. An activity is an element of work for which one person is responsible.*

The Task & Activity List is the means by which the Project Leader's exerts day-to-day control over project progress. It can be created using software such as MS-Project or even a spreadsheet. However it is created, the same information should be shown:

- Sequence Number - a phase is identified by a one-part number, a task by two-part number - Phase.Task - an activity by a full three-part number - Phase.Task.Activity

- Description

  - A phase is a group of tasks ending at a milestone and, for ease of recognition should be capitalised and emboldened

  - A task is set of closely related activities that specifies a distinct piece of work within a phase and which should be capitalised

  - An activity is an element of work for which one person is responsible and starts with a verb, and which should be in lower case

- Responsibility - is assigned only to activities and identifies the person responsible for the completion of the activity. The person responsible is typically the Project Team Member of the relevant domain but may be any project role. Other people may do the work for which the person is responsible.

- Target Date - the date by which the activity is expected to be complete. This date cannot be entered until the estimating and scheduling is complete. Target dates should fit within any given deadlines.

- Estimated Effort - the effort of the person responsible for activity completion - if teams are involved, the effort of the teams should be converted to a cost and shown in the Cost Estimate, and the cost either invoiced or cross-charged to the project by the supplier

- Status – when complete an activity is marked with 'C'. The notion of 'percentage complete' is at best irrelevant and at worst misleading. If an activity is no longer required as the result of a change request, it should be marked N – don't erase it.

Note that the Task & Activity List does not include a 'start date' column. This is because in practice the start of an activity is rarely dependant on the final completion of a preceding activity – if it is, take this into account in negotiating the target date. A 'start date' is at best irrelevant and at worst restraining.

Steps

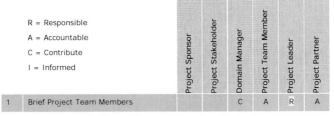

		Project Sponsor	Project Stakeholder	Domain Manager	Project Team Member	Project Leader	Project Partner
1	Brief Project Team Members			C	A	R	A

The Project Leader should bring each Project Team Member 'up to speed'. This can be done individually but is best done as a group.

It's reasonable to expect each Project Team Member to read the Project Definition and the Cost Benefit Analysis, and essential for them to understand the Phase Plan, the Precedence Diagram and the Deliverable Log, as well as the specifications, development methods, and quality standards relevant to them.

| 2 | Retrieve & incorporate templates | | | C | R | A | A |

The Project Leader and each Project Team Member should seek templates – Task & Activity Lists for similar, previous projects from the Knowledge Library that can be used to guide the creation of the deliverables for this project.

| 3 | Detail tasks and activities for each deliverable | | | C | R | A | A |

The creation of a deliverable is controlled by planning the detailed tasks and activities in a section of the Task & Activity List.

The Task & Activity List is best built as a series of 'checkpoint activities'. These are used by the Project Leader to maintain control over the progress of the deliverable creation rather than to explain how to do the creative work.

Each task should have at least one activity. Write activity descriptions as an instruction and keep them brief – if a lengthy description is needed include it in the Requirements Specification which supports the deliverable.

About ten checkpoint activities should be sufficient to maintain control over most deliverables. However, plan according to your confidence level in the supplier - if you are not confident or it is a supplier with whom you have not worked before, increase the number of checkpoint activities.

Where R = Responsible, A = Accountable, C = Contribute, I = Informed

If you need to explain how to do the creative work or tasks need to be coordinated on a time and sequence critical basis, for example, a critical machine move, use the Minute-by-Minute Schedule to further plan this detail – don't clutter the Task & Activity List.

Insert 'decision point activities' into the plan where there is a choice about future direction, content or structure of the project.

The Project Leader can either work with each Project Team Member to build the Task & Activity List or delegate responsibility to a Project Team Member.

The Project Team Member can then work with subject matter experts within the domain to plan what has to be done and then agree the checkpoint activities with the Project Leader.

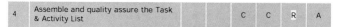

4	Assemble and quality assure the Task & Activity List			C	C	R	A

The Project Leader assembles the sections into a complete Task & Activity List in accordance with the Deliverable Log, Precedence Diagram and Phase Plan.

The Project Leader and Project Partner should then read through the Task & Activity List to check that:

- It is logical and complete

- Any jargon is defined in the project's Glossary of Terms

- It adheres to 'common sense'.

If any deficiencies are found, then return to step 1.

Planning for iterations

It is important to be realistic when planning – only simple deliverables can be created right first time. Plan iterations of work and quality assurance based on both:

- Complexity of the work, as assessed by a subject matter expert:

		Score
Simple	'Run of the mill'	1
Moderate	Needs judgement	2
Complex	Out of the ordinary	3
Very complex	Would tax an expert	4

- The skill and experience of those doing the work:

		Score
Beginner	Never done it before	5
Developing	Had training but little experience	4
Maturing	Some experience	3
Mature	Extensive and varied experience	2
Expert	Recognised as an authority	1

The best estimate for the number of iterations required to create a deliverable is the product of the two scores. Iterations should be shown on the Task & Activity List, so that realistic estimates are made. Each iteration or cluster of iterations should have a creation activity and a quality control activity.

Task & Activity Detailing Checklist

1	Is there a section of Task & Activity List for each deliverable explaining what has to be done to create the deliverable?
2	Are sufficient 'checkpoint activities' included in relation to your confidence in the supplier?
3	Do all activity descriptions start with a verb?
4	Has any detailed information about deliverables and quality standards been included in a Requirements Specification?
5	Are Minute-by-Minute Schedules needed in support of the Task & Activity List?
6	Are 'decision point' activities included where needed?
7	Have sufficient iterations been allowed in relation to the complexity of the deliverables and the skill and experience of the people doing the work?
8	Does each cycle of work include a quality assurance activity?
9	Are these sections assembled into a complete Task & Activity List?
10	Has the Task & Activity List been quality assured by the Project Leader and Partner?

Team Planning

Steps

		Project Sponsor	Project Stakeholder	Domain Manager	Project Team Member	Project Leader	Project Partner
	R = Responsible						
	A = Accountable						
	C = Contribute						
	I = Informed						
1	Circulate Task & Activity List			I	I	R	A

Once it is assembled as a quality document, a copy of the complete Task & Activity List should be given to each Project Team Member.

| 2 | Team Planning Session | I | | C | A | R | A |

The purpose of the team planning session is to eliminate any errors and omissions from the Task & Activity List and to hone it - there will be instances where minor changes can improve the quality beyond measure – these can only be identified by the team working together.

During team planning, ownership transfer of the plans to the project team is achieved by:

- Inviting their comments and criticisms

- Hearing and listening to what they say

- Incorporating their ideas.

Allow effort in the Task & Activity List for necessary reviews, audits and meetings – taking into account the duration of meetings and number of attendees.

3	Revise the Task & Activity List			C	C	R	A

After each team planning session, the Project Leader should create a new version of the Task & Activity List.

If either the Project Leader or Project Partner feels more improvements are possible, return to step 1.

Team Planning Checklist

1	Does each Project Team Member have a copy of the current Task & Activity List?
2	Has ownership transfer of the Task & Activity List taken place whereby the team perception is one of 'us working on our plans'?
3	Have you allowed for necessary reviews, audits and meetings?
4	Is the Task & Activity List of acceptable quality?

Estimating & Scheduling

Steps

R = Responsible A = Accountable C = Contribute I = Informed	Project Sponsor	Project Stakeholder	Domain Manager	Project Team Member	Project Leader	Project Partner
1	Estimate effort activity by activity			C	A	R	C

The Project Leader and the Project Team Member will both know which section of the Task & Activity List describes the work that will create which deliverable. Activities should cover checkpoints, decision points, planned number of iterations, quality assurance activities, audits, reviews, meetings and reporting.

For each activity, the Project Leader and Project Team Member should separately estimate the effort needed and then compare notes. In most cases the effort required will be easily agreed. As a guideline, no work activity should exceed five days effort before introducing a checkpoint activity, and there must be at least one checkpoint activity per Project Team Member each week.

Where consensus cannot be easily reached, negotiate a 'win-win' outcome, agree to break the activity into more, smaller activities or consult with a subject matter expert.

During these sessions, the Project Leader should identify probable expenditure and populate the Cost Estimate relevant to the deliverables, to include people, tools and materials. The estimate, of both effort and cost, is part of the delivery promise the Project Leader is seeking.

2	Negotiate activity target dates	C		C	A	R	A

For each estimated activity, the Project Leader should add the relevant target dates. Target dates, if necessary, may be adjusted to suit people's diaries but milestones and key deliverable deadlines cannot be moved.

The target date is part of the delivery promise the Project Leader is seeking for each activity.

3	Confirm Task & Activity List	I		A	C	R	A

When the Task & Activity List is complete convert the nodes on the Precedence Diagram to milestones by inserting the final target date within each Phase.

4	Confirm manpower, costs & benefits					R	A

The Project Leader should compile the Cost Estimate and Manpower Estimate from the completed Task & Activity List and add on any percentage contingency allowance – see Risk Management.

With the agreement of the Project Sponsor, the manpower and costs of the Cost Benefit Analysis should be updated, and the manpower and cost margin of error adjusted in line with the contingency allowance.

The Project Sponsor should now have all the information needed to support the Bid for full funding:

- A Project Definition with assumptions replaced by clear decisions

- A Precedence Diagram with milestones - a Gantt Chart can also be produced at this time that accurately reflects achievable milestone dates

- A completely planned, estimated and scheduled Task & Activity List

- A Cost Benefit Analysis verified by the Benefit Plan, Cost Estimate and Manpower Estimate

- A comprehensive Risk Log including all mitigating actions agreed with the Project Sponsor from the evaluations of the risks

If the Project Leader and Project Partner are not completely satisfied with the project plan, they should act to correct the deficiency.

Estimating & Scheduling Checklist

1	Has a 'win-win' estimate of effort, cost and target date been negotiated for all activities?
2	Have all project management activities been estimated and given target dates?
3	Have all assumptions been replaced by clear decisions?
4	Have all known risks been evaluated and appropriate mitigating actions and contingency plans put in place?
5	Has a contingency allowance been decided and applied?
6	Are all planning and control documents quality and complete?
7	Can the project be delivered as promised using the manpower, money and time set out in the Bid for full funding?

Agreement

Steps

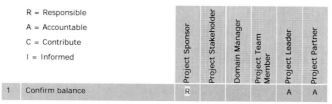

		Project Sponsor	Project Stakeholder	Domain Manager	Project Team Member	Project Leader	Project Partner
	R = Responsible						
	A = Accountable						
	C = Contribute						
	I = Informed						
1	Confirm balance	R				A	A

The Project Sponsor may reasonably challenge any part of the plan from a benefits realisation perspective. At the same time, the Project Leader should be able to defend every part of the plan from a delivery perspective.

If planning has exposed deficiencies then the original Bid was inadequate – in short the project will fail unless the full funding is increased.

The Project Leader should not try to conceal the need for an increase in funding, 'the truth will out' in time anyway!

| 2 | Confirm viability and affordability, and make Go/Nogo decision | R | | | | A | A |

The Project Sponsor can only authorise Project Delivery if the project is viable and affordable and this has been agreed with the Executive Sponsor.

The Head of Demand should also confirm that the project is viable and affordable before the revised Bid is submitted to the Change Board for full funding.

| 3 | Submit Bid for sanction of full-funding | R | | | | A | A |

Dependent upon the decision, the Project Leader should:

- Proceed to Project Delivery if the Bid is approved and full funding granted
- Re-scope, starting again at Project Inception with initial funding
- Terminate and close the project

| 4 | Sign contracts | R | I | A | | A | A |

The plan for Project Delivery should now be complete. If the project is sanctioned, the Project Leader can proceed with the signing of supplier contracts in accordance with organisation policy and processes.

Agreement Checklist

1	Is the plan complete and can its contents be defended against challenge?
2	Has the Bid been updated with the Manpower Estimate and Cost Estimate?
3	Is the plan complete to a level whereby the Project Sponsor is confident to apply to the Executive Sponsor and Change Board for full funding?
4	Has the Head of Change confirmed viability and affordability?
5	Has a formal 'Go–no go' decision been made by the Executive Sponsor and sanction for full funding obtained from the Change Board?

Tips

- Negotiate service agreements with internal suppliers and contracts with external suppliers, and agree each supplier's Terms of Business

- Ensure that Requirements Specifications form part of the supplier agreement or contract

- Detailed planning is a 'two-person lift'

- Planning is best done in a series of sprints not as a marathon

- When you are planning, invent ways of reducing interruption from business-as-usual so you can concentrate, for example: 'Red Hats', off-site working, delegating your day-job

- The Project Leader should avoid, wherever possible, taking responsibility for doing project work – project management activity should keep them busy!

- It is inevitable that issues and new sensitivities will be identified during Detailed Planning - the Project Leader should ensure rapid resolution of issues, evaluate sensitivities and, if a risk, add it to the Risk Log

- Recommend to the Project Sponsor that a project is re-scoped or terminated if it is not viable or there are insufficient resources - do not fight a battle you cannot win.

Project Delivery

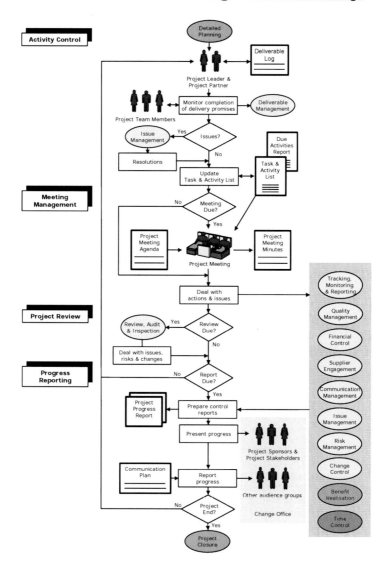

Figure 17: Project Delivery Process Map

Project Delivery is the process that manages the promises made by Project Team Members and applies the agreed tracking, monitoring, and reporting processes to ensure the project is delivered according to plan. It can start when the Change Board has approved full funding.

Creation of deliverables is managed through Deliverable Management.

> *In a well-planned project, if you're fortunate, Project Delivery is little more than 'ticking off' complete activities and deliverables. For the most part, there will be unplanned actions, many issues, change requests and adverse outcome risks. Keep on your toes and maintain communications!*

Activity Control

Steps

		Project Sponsor	Project Stakeholder	Domain Manager	Project Team Member	Project Leader	Project Partner
	R = Responsible A = Accountable C = Contribute I = Informed						
1	Monitor delivery promise completion			I	A	R	A

At least once a week, the Project Leader should meet 'one-to-one' with each Project Team Member – armed with the latest Due Activities Report - those activities in the Task & Activity List, the target dates of which are earlier than a specific date, used to expedite their completion. The conversation, if you have planned well, is short and sweet - Project Leader: "Are you on track to complete your due activities this week?" Project Team Member: "Yes".

2	Issues?	C	C	A	A	R	A

It is inevitable that the answer will sometimes be: "No". In this context, if the activities are not 'on track', there is an issue and if left unresolved it will cause slippage.

> *Slippage is an amount of time, money or manpower over and above that estimated for the completion of a project phase, brought about by an issue.*

In such situations the Project Leader should apply the Issue Management process. For the most part, addressing circumstances in a firm but courteous manner, will achieve a rapid and satisfactory resolution. Occasionally, however, a Project Team Member will have a major problem. These situations should be dealt with as a matter of urgency – see 'Removing obstacles'.

3	Update Task & Activity List				C	R	A

A dedicated Project Leader has no excuse for letting the Task & Activity List or the Deliverable Log become out-of-date. It's best to update documents daily.

Removing obstacles

> **Projects slip 'one day at a time' - it is less stressful to deal quickly with an issue than to recover from one left to fester!**

A Project Team Member may be prevented from keeping a delivery promise because:

- An unexpected circumstance has occurred or an assumption has been refuted – a resolution should be negotiated with the person or the issue raised by the Project Leader to the relevant domain manger

- Of a loss of empowerment – this occurs most frequently because their manager has reneged on the commitment to the project. In which case, the manager becomes the Project Leader's focus of an issue

- They are struggling to complete the work through having underestimated the effort required or a lack of personal capability, or confidence. The Project Leader should help, either directly or by using a subject matter expert. If this fails, and with the person's agreement, a resolution should be negotiated with their manager.

If a person becomes uncooperative or even disruptive, the Project Leader should eliminate any possible causes above, and then apply the 'three strikes' guideline:

- First occurrence – communicate your dissatisfaction to the person, giving the reasons

- Second occurrence – escalate an issue to the relevant domain manger

- Third occurrence – ask the domain manager to replace the person – which, if refused, the Project Leader should escalate as an issue to the Project Sponsor.

Activity Control Checklist

1	Are you having one-to-one sessions at least once a week with each Project Team Member?
2	Are you dealing with late activities immediately?
3	Are you confronting 'threat of broken promise' issues?
4	Are you updating the planning and control documents daily?

Meeting Management

Steps

	Project Sponsor	Project Stakeholder	Domain Manager	Project Team Member	Project Leader	Project Partner
R = Responsible A = Accountable C = Contribute I = Informed						
1 Meeting due?	I	I	I	C	R	A

Project meetings should be scheduled for each week. The day before each meeting, the Project Leader should circulate the meeting agenda to the members and any others who may be asked to attend - see Project Meeting Agenda.

External suppliers who are Project Team Members should not be excluded because of sensitive issues on the agenda. Sensitive issues are best dealt with in separate meetings.

Maintain a spirit of 'camaraderie' within the team by valuing each person and treating them as a professional. Act to avoid the formation of 'us and them' situations between internal and external suppliers.

2 Project meeting	I	I	I	A	R	A

A project meeting need not be a lengthy affair – aim for no more than one hour and go armed with the current Due Activities Report.

The Project Leader should chair the meeting with the Project Partner, or someone selected by the Project Leader, taking the minutes – see Project Meeting Minutes.

3 Deal with actions and issues	C	C	A	A	R	A

A project meeting produces three types of output:

* Decisions that needs to be communicated

* Actions for which someone present, who is empowered to do so, makes a delivery promise

* Issues to be resolved – an action for the Project Leader.

An action that is not completed as promised is a blockage to progress, to which the Project Leader should apply Issue Management.

Project Meeting Agenda

1 Previous Minutes (purpose of meeting for inaugural meeting) – this monitors the completion of actions agreed at previous meetings

2 Tasks & Activities

The Project Leader should ask each Project Team Member in turn if all due activities are complete. If the answer is "Yes", then the Project Leader should ask to see the evidence. If the answer is "No" or evidence cannot be presented, the activity becomes subject to Issue Management

3   Reviews

- Issues - The purpose is to find a quick and easy resolution – and failing that to formulate the issue, which the Project Leader will escalate

- Risks - The purpose is to monitor the status of all know risks and to identify new sensitivities which the Project Leader will assess and, if necessary, organise a Risk Workshop

- Changes - The purpose is to agree how approved change requests will be implemented. New change requests are validated and impact assessed as and when they arise, not in a project meeting

4   Forecasts of milestones, key deliverables, manpower, costs and benefits

These are additional checks that all is 'on track'. The Project Leader should insist on 'no surprises'; if something is off track, then the Project Team Member should inform the Project Leader before the meeting so that it can be dealt with as an issue

5   Any other business (only if agreed in advance)

In practice, these are matters that could be more easily and better dealt with in smaller, special-purpose meeting. Avoid whenever possible.

Project Meeting Minutes

It is best to number minutes consecutively through the entire series of project meetings.

Actions are only placed on anyone present at the meeting.

It is best if the Project Meeting Minutes are taken 'on line' using a 'laptop' PC with the wording of each minute agreed. This obviates the otherwise inevitable requests for amendment, much effort is saved and the minutes can be circulated immediately the meeting is concluded.

Meeting Management Checklist

1	Are you having Project meeting once a week with each Project Team Member present?
2	Are you circulating the Project Meeting Agenda the day before the meeting?
3	Do your Project Meetings keep to the agenda and end within an hour?
4	Are your Project Meeting Minutes no more than a list of decisions, actions for those present, and issues for you to escalate?
5	Are your Project Meeting Minutes circulated immediately the meeting is concluded?

Project Review

A review is an examination of the conduct and performance of a project, at any time, in relation to the organisation's project management processes and quality standards.

An audit is an examination of the probity.

An inspection is an unscheduled examination of the compliance, of a project in relation to:

- Legal or regulatory requirements

- Industry standards

- Organisation's quality standards.

Steps

R = Responsible

A = Accountable

C = Contribute

I = Informed

		Project Sponsor	Project Stakeholder	Domain Manager	Project Team Member	Project Leader	Project Partner
1	Review due?	I	I	I	I	R	A

For the most part reviews and audits will have been scheduled during Detailed Planning; inspections tend to be unscheduled. Any preparatory work needed in advance of a review or audit will have been scheduled in the Task & Activity List during Detailed Planning – in practice, there should be little such work; a well-managed project is 'all but' ready for review or audit at any time.

A well-managed project is 'all but' ready for an inspection at any time.

2	Review, Audit & Inspection	C	C	C	C	R	A

Any review, audit or inspection will absorb people's effort – if the work has been scheduled in the Task & Activity List, there is no consequence. However, an unscheduled audit or inspection can absorb so much effort that it represents a blockage to progress – and so becomes an issue.

3	Deal with risks, issues & changes	C	C	A	A	R	A

Any review, audit or inspection produces three types of outcome:

- Risks that needs to be evaluated

- Issues that need to be resolved

- Change requests that need to be evaluated and approved and, to all intents and purposes, will be mandatory.

The responsibility for each is with the Project Leader.

Review Checklist

1	Is the work associated with all known reviews, audits and inspections scheduled in the Task & Activity List?

2	Are your planning and control documents up-to-date – and do they 'tell the story' of a well-managed project?

Progress Reporting

Steps

		Project Sponsor	Project Stakeholder	Domain Manager	Project Team Member	Project Leader	Project Partner
R = Responsible							
A = Accountable							
C = Contribute							
I = Informed							
1	Report due?				I	R	A

The activities required prompt progress reporting would have been scheduled in the Task & Activity List during Detailed Planning. In practice, these activities should amount to little work; in a well-managed project, reports are easily produced and circulated.

| 2 | Prepare control reports | C | C | C | C | R | A |

There are nine reports that the Project Sponsor, during shaping of the project, may have asked to be circulated. The Project Sponsor may instead have opted for the 'summary on a page' Progress Report. In either case, the Project Leader will find it advantageous and easy to produce the individual reports for personal reference if nothing else.

| 3 | Present progress | A | A | I | I | R | A |

A regular, ideally weekly, meeting of the Project Sponsor and Project Leader will have been scheduled during Detailed Planning.

If the Project Sponsor elected during shaping of the project to have a Steering Committee, this meeting will be attended by selected Project Stakeholders and will be more formal. In practice, few projects need a Steering Committee – they are only really appropriate to programmes.

In whatever form the meeting is held, the agenda is the same – see Project Sponsor Meeting below

| 4 | Report progress | A | A | I | I | R | A |

During the meeting with the Project Sponsor, the progress of the Communication Plan should also be reported.

Reports

The recommended colour coding for use in all progress reports is:

Completed	Target achieved
To plan	On track for delivery as promised
At risk	Because of unresolved issues or significant risks
Slipped	Irrecoverable slippage

A 'summary on a page' Progress Report can be circulated in place of individual reports – but the Project Leader should produce them anyway.

Milestone Report

The Milestone Report states the planned, forecast and actual dates for completion of the phases of a project – with brief reasons for any variance. A red milestone should have a corresponding entry on the Issue List.

Issue List

The Issue List brings issues for which resolutions have not been provided in a timely manner to the attention of the Project Sponsor, Steering Committee and Change Board. An issue is put on the Issue List if its resolution is being blocked or unduly delayed and lack of a rapid resolution will cause, or has caused, irrecoverable slippage. Once the issue has been resolved it is removed from the Issue List.

Risk Log

The Risk Log is the definitive record of risks throughout the life of a project. It describes each risk, shows its status, type and severity, and briefly describes any mitigating actions or contingency plan.

Key Deliverable Report

The Key Deliverable Report states the planned, forecast and actual dates for completion of key deliverables – with brief reasons for any variance. A red key deliverable should have a corresponding entry on the Issue List.

Cost Control

The Cost Control report states the originally planned, currently planned, and actual costs incurred by a projects – with brief reasons for any variance. Costs incurred in excess of current plan are slippage.

Manpower Control

The Manpower Control report states the variance between estimated and actual manpower used on a project. It is inevitable that in detail estimated and actual manpower will be different – overall, the actual manpower should be kept within the limits agreed when full funding was granted. Use of manpower in excess of current plan is slippage.

Change Log

The Change Log is the definitive record of changes to any aspect of the programme or project. It describes

each change request, shows its impact, and states the
Project Sponsor's approve/defer/reject decision.

Critical Success Factor Log

The Critical Success Factor Log is inventory of critical
success factors current in the project. It shows the
significant entities, which must be within limits in order
to achieve success.

Benefit Report

The Benefit Report states the originally planned,
currently planned and actual realisation of benefits of an
initiative with brief reasons for any actual or expected
variance.

Project Sponsor Meeting

Although this meeting is informal, the Project Leader should
note all decisions and actions. The subjects to be covered
include:

- During definition and planning:
  - The benefits Project Sponsor is seeking
  - The changes that need to be made
  - The impact on the organisation
  - Which options, if more than one, to pursue
  - The preferred option.
- During delivery and closure:
  - Progress against milestones and the specific issues
    relating to any slippage
  - Related events happening outside the project
  - Realisation of benefits.

Progress Reporting Checklist

1	Are all reporting activities scheduled in the Task & Activity List?
2	Do you have up-to-date copies of the control reports, even if they aren't to be circulated?
3	Are you meeting at least once a week with the Project Sponsor?
4	Are you covering the intended agenda when you meet with your Project Sponsor?

Tips

- The purpose of a plan is to know if you are deviating from plan, so you can get back on plan or re-plan

- Look forward in order to identify issues and take corrective action to resolve them before they block progress

- Enforce promises - deal immediately and appropriately with the threat of broken promises by identifying and resolving the issue

- Target dates can be altered only as a result of an approved change - however, don't expect all activity target dates to be achieved but instead focus on encouraging people to make up any lost ground before milestone and key deliverable dates are impacted

- Be honest – if a milestone or key deliverable date is missed, don't try to hide it but expect the Project Sponsor to question it

- Be alert to possible opportunities to improve on the plan

- Avoid 90% complete syndrome by using the 'show-me' technique

- Take every opportunity to praise achievement

- Communicate and celebrate genuine success

- Whenever in doubt, ask!

Project Closure

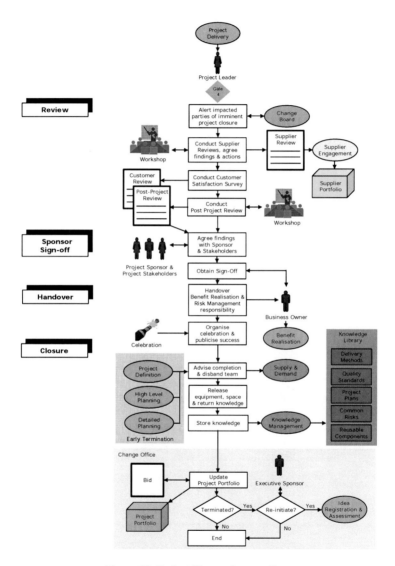

Figure 18: Project Closure Process Map

Project Closure starts either when Project Delivery is complete, the deliverables have been 'signed-off' and handed over or when the project has been terminated early at some stage following Project Inception. Project Closure is the process that:

- Disengages the people assigned to the project
- Archives re-usable knowledge in the Knowledge Library
- Formally ends all work and expenditure on the project.

> *Project Closure is the end of the project for the Project Leader, Project Partner, Domain Controllers and Project Team Members.*
>
> *The Project Sponsor role ends but the holder of this role continues as Business Owner until all planned benefits have been realised.*
>
> *A Project Stakeholder's responsibilities also continue either in the role of Benefit Owner or as the manager of Benefit Owners.*

As soon as the work of a domain is ended, that part of the project may advance to Project Closure.

Review

Steps

		Project Sponsor	Project Stakeholder	Domain Manager	Project Team Member	Project Leader	Project Partner
	R = Responsible A = Accountable C = Contribute I = Informed						
1	Alert impacted parties to imminent closure of project	I	I	I	I	R	A

Advise the Executive Sponsor and Change Board that the project is ended and obtain permission to close. Project Closure will come as no surprise. Nevertheless, people do need warning and others told directly – especially the finance function, which will want to close the project cost centre.

| 2 | Conduct supplier reviews, agree findings and actions | I | I | A | C | R | A |

Any supplier performance measurement criteria agreed in Supplier Engagement will be monitored throughout Project Delivery and any deviations attended to by the Project Leader through the escalation process. The Supplier Review tool is used to record the actions and decisions from a review of supplier performance at the end of a project. The supplier review itself is a workshop which answers three questions:

- What went well – and should be repeated in the future
- What went badly – and should be avoided in the future
- What should be done to strengthen the relationship.

The Supplier Review should be stored in the Supplier Portfolio of the relevant business-as-usual function.

3	Conduct Customer Satisfaction Survey	A	A	C	C	R	A

The Customer Review tool is the report of the customer satisfaction survey. The customer satisfaction survey gathers the customers' opinion of the:

- Quality, timeliness and cost of the deliverables
- The effectiveness of the relationship between the customer domain and the Project Team.

4	Conduct post-project review	A	A	C	C	R	A

The Post-Project Review tool is simply a report of the workshop findings. It is best done with the knowledge of all Customer Reviews. Whilst the workshop is the responsibility of the Project Leader, an independent facilitator and co-facilitator should be engaged.

Post-Project Review

The Post-Project Review shows how the project met, exceeded or fell short of its success criteria by answering the following questions:

- How does the completed project fit current business needs and stakeholder expectations?
- To what extent were the project objectives met?
- What is the status of the critical success factors?
- To what extent did the project stay within its agreed scope?
- How were the expectations of the Project Sponsor and Project Stakeholders satisfied?
- To what extent do the deliverables match their specifications and quality standards?
- To what extent did the project stay within its agreed timescales?
- How does actual manpower used compare with that planned?
- How do actual costs compare with those planned?
- To what extent has the project enabled the realisation of the anticipated benefits?
- What project activities remain outstanding?
- What issues remain outstanding?
- What risks remain outstanding?
- What changes remain?
- What administration activities remain outstanding?

Review Checklist

1	Have all impacted parties been alerted to the imminent project closure?
2	Have all Supplier Reviews been completed and the results agreed, actioned and stored in the Supplier Portfolio?
3	Is a customer satisfaction survey needed and have all Customer Reviews been completed and the results analysed?
4	Has an independent facilitator and co-facilitator been engaged for the post-project review workshop?
5	Has the content of the Post-Project Review been agreed with the Project Sponsor and Project Stakeholders?
6	Is the Post-Project Review complete?

Sponsor Sign-Off

Steps

R = Responsible
A = Accountable
C = Contribute
I = Informed

		Project Sponsor	Project Stakeholder	Domain Manager	Project Team Member	Project Leader	Project Partner
1	Agree findings with Project Sponsor and Project Stakeholders	A	A			R	A

The Post-Project Review will indicate possible improvements to the way in which future projects are conducted and where individual performance can be improved.

Most importantly, it will identify any work that was ruled out of scope and change requests that were deferred, which may need to be the focus of another initiative.

| 2 | Obtain sign-off | A | I | I | | R | A |

The Project Leader is responsible for obtaining sign-off. Sign-off means that the Business Owner will, at an agreed time, take over responsibility for all aspects of benefit realisation and the management of any operational risks.

It also give the Project Leader authority to disband the Project Team, release all equipment and office space, hand-over relevant documents and tools to the Knowledge Library, and to organise the end-of project celebration!

Sign-off Checklist

1	Has the Post-Project Review been agreed by the Project Leader, Project Partner, Project Sponsor and Project Stakeholders?
2	Does the Business Owner have the Benefit Plan, Benefit Report and Risk Log, and understand all remaining open risks and activities?

Handover

Steps

		Project Sponsor	Project Stakeholder	Domain Manager	Project Team Member	Project Leader	Project Partner
R = Responsible A = Accountable C = Contribute I = Informed							
1	Handover benefit realisation & risk management responsibility	A				R	A

Handover and acceptance should be formally recorded. It is probably best if the handover meeting is minuted. The Project Leader and Project Partner can look forward to their next assignment.

| 2 | Arrange for benefit monitoring | A | I | I | | R | A |

Benefits that are not measured and monitored are seldom realised. The people empowered to change measures and targets in the Benefit Plan should apply them to the organisation's budgets and performance targets.

| 3 | Organise celebration and publicise success | A | C | C | C | R | A |

Projects come to a planned but abrupt end. Many people will have contributed knowledge, skills, experience, and 'blood, sweat and tears' to make the project a success - it's worth a party!

> *Don't just wait until the end of a project to celebrate - have a small celebration when each major milestone is achieved - recognise and reward exemplary performance as and when it occurs – treat people as you would wish to be treated! Publicise success at the end of the project.*

Projects deliver change, change that improves the performance of the organisation, something about which the organisation can be proud – it's also worth telling people inside and outside the organisation.

Handover Checklist

1	Has the Business Owner received all relevant documents to enable them to fulfil their post-project responsibilities?
2	Has handover to the Business Owner taken place and acceptance confirmed?
3	Have the minutes of the handover meeting, or meetings, been agreed?
4	Has an appropriate celebration been organised with the right people invited?
5	Has the success been publicised in-line with organisational policy?

Closure

If a project is terminated early, the Executive Director and Change Board will have agreed and it joins the Project Closure process at this point.

Steps

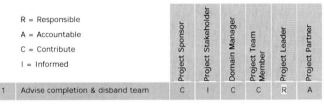

		Project Sponsor	Project Stakeholder	Domain Manager	Project Team Member	Project Leader	Project Partner
1	Advise completion & disband team	C	I	C	C	R	A

Advise finance that the project cost centre should be closed, once the final invoices have been approved for payment.

The Change Office's Supply & Demand process will require information about people's skills, knowledge, experience, and performance. The Project Sponsor and Project Leader can supply this information.

Thank each Project Team Member and let the manager of their domain know. Written 'bouquets' are valuable assets for people seeking new challenges. People will often ask for references, which should not be unreasonably refused.

The Project Leader should ask the Business Owner to assess their performance during the course of the project and complete an End of Assignment Report. This is fed into the organisation's performance management process.

2	Release equipment, space and return knowledge	I				R	A

Ensure that confidential information belonging to third parties is returned to the owner or disposed of securely by agreement, and intellectual property returned to its rightful owner. This is little more than good housekeeping - and a legal obligation.

3	Store knowledge	I				R	A

Much will have been learned during the project, knowledge from which the organisation and its people can gain advantage. Specifications, quality standards, development methods and reusable components should be prepared, stored and indexed for easy retrieval in the Knowledge Library.

4	Update project portfolio	I				R	A

Agree with the Business Owner what they intend to do with any de-scoped work and deferred change requests remaining on the Change Log. Action might include generation of a new Bid or handover to the Business Owner for action through continual improvement.

Tips

- Don't skimp on project closure
- Avoid loose ends – make sure that everything is handed over to someone who accepts responsibility
- Thank all who have made the project a success – say it to them and write to them
- When you reward exemplary performance, do it with panache!

Benefit Planning

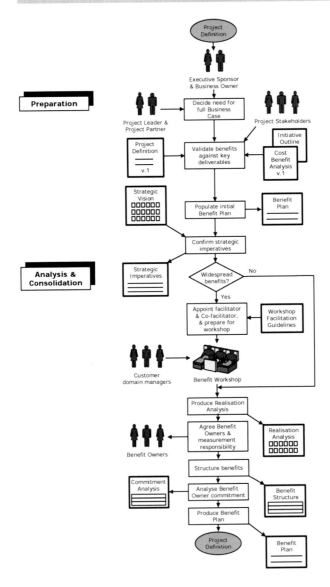

Figure 19: Benefit Planning Process Map

Benefit Planning provides the linkage between Project Management and Value Management. It is the process that:

- Links anticipated benefits through project or programme objectives to the company's strategic imperatives
- Identifies the specific changes that will enable benefit realisation
- Makes the realisation of each benefit the responsibility of a named 'Benefit Owner'
- Establishes responsibility for measuring the realisation of each benefit.

> **A benefit is the measurable added value anticipated from the completion of a project.**

Benefits are realised when the business-as-usual of a customer domain is changed so that value is added to the organisation.

Benefits can be:

- Financial – having a measurable impact on the organisation's profit & loss account or balance sheet
- Non-financial – any other.

Every project must enable benefits but not every project will realise financial benefits. The organisation will welcome non-financial benefits, providing they are ones that it is specifically seeking.

The process of planning benefits begins with the preparation of a Bid for resources by the Business Owner and approval of initial funding by the Change Board. Anticipated benefits are set out in the Cost Benefit Analysis section of the Bid.

Preparation

Steps

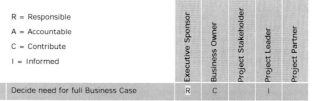

		Executive Sponsor	Business Owner	Project Stakeholder	Project Leader	Project Partner
R = Responsible A = Accountable C = Contribute I = Informed						
1	Decide need for full Business Case	R	C		I	

The Executive Sponsor may decide that a full Business Case is needed to gain Change Board commitment.

A Business Case is the justification of an investment and the allocation of sufficient resources, so that its worth can be reviewed in the context of strategy and impact on the organisation - it contains a Cost Benefit Analysis and Investment Appraisal.

This should be a deliverable from the project and prepared whilst project planning is taking place.

2	Validate benefits against key deliverables	C	R	C	A	

Anticipated benefits are validated following the Project Definition process and confirmation of the key deliverables.

If there are doubts about the key deliverables, the requirements or features, Benefit Planning can be delayed until after High Level Planning has advanced.

It is the features of each key deliverable that will trigger advantages and benefits. 'Things can only get better when people do things differently' – therefore, faster, more accurate, more accessible, better formatted and more current are features but never benefits.

Analysis of the features will determine the anticipated benefits. Be sure to include everything that will grow the business, cut costs, save time, fix infrastructure or reduce exposure to risk.

Once you are satisfied that the list is complete, prove the validity and significance of each benefit using the following tests:

- 'Which means that' Test

  The organisation's primary interest is in measurable benefits. To distinguish benefits from advantages, apply the 'which means that' test. For example, when you have decided what you think a benefit might be – say, 'increased sales', 'improved morale', 'lower costs', 'more efficiency' – apply the test. If you conclude that it can be taken no further then you have arrived at the benefit. If this matches a benefit you know the organisation is seeking then it is worthy of inclusion in the Benefit Plan.

- 'So what' Test

  Having identified the benefit, the significance to the organisation can be assessed by applying the 'so what' test. If a measurable difference is significant then people will be interested and it should be included in the Benefit Plan. If not, it's best to exclude it.

Avoid counting cost avoidance benefits as financial benefits, for example, "If we don't do such and such then this will happen and it will cost us this much". Cost avoidance does not impact the organisation's profit & loss account or balance sheet and is therefore a non-financial benefit as far as the project is concerned.

3	Populate initial Benefit Plan	R	C	A	I	

Enter the valid benefits on the Benefit Plan.

4	Confirm strategic imperatives	R	C		I	

The strategic imperatives of the organisation need to be confirmed by the Business Owner before realisation analysis can commence.

If a Strategic Vision document exists, the strategic imperatives should be found within.

Preparation Checklist

1	Are the anticipated benefits complete?
2	Is each benefit both valid and significant?
3	Are the strategic imperatives the primary focus of the organisation and is each one an essential requirement of it delivering its strategy?

Analysis & Consolidation

Required inputs are the Initiative Details, the Cost Benefit Analysis and the Project Definition. The primary output is the Benefit Plan.

Benefit Plan

The Benefit Plan lists each financial and non-financial benefit, identifies the Benefit Owners – customer domain managers and Project Stakeholders - and the people who will measure them. Production of the Benefit Plan is the responsibility of the Project Sponsor in their capacity of Business Owner.

Realisation Analysis

The **Realisation Analysis** is used to relate the organisation's strategic imperatives to the objectives from the **Project Definition** and the benefits from the **Cost Benefit Analysis**, so as to identify the necessary:

- *Changes required to enable benefit realisation*

- *Enablers that make change possible*

- *Components of enablers.*

The elements of the Realisation Analysis are:

- Strategic imperatives - the topics that are presently the primary focus of the organisation and which is an essential requirement of delivering its strategy.

- Objectives - a targeted achievement of the project or programme aimed at the initiative purpose and against which it will be measured.

- Benefits - the measurable added value anticipated from the completion of work - it is realised when the business-as-usual of a customer domain is changed such that value is added to the organisation.

- Changes - events used to alter favourably the state of something; they involve creating, integrating or transforming the capabilities, enablers and assets of an organisation, which include people, processes and systems. It describes the difference between the existing business-as-usual and that required for at least one of the anticipated benefits to be realised.

- Enablers – a pre-requisite for at least one required change.

- Components - part, or a detail, of an enabler or change.

The identified changes will enable the Project Leader to quickly and accurately validate the project's key deliverables.

Steps

R = Responsible

A = Accountable

C = Contribute

I = Informed

		Business Owner	Project Stekeholder	Project Leader	Project Partner	Benefit Owner
1	Widespread benefits?	R	C	I	I	C

If the project involves many customer domains and wide-ranging benefits, formulation of a Benefit Plan may require a Benefit Workshop. This is decided by the Benefit Owner - see guidelines below.

| 2 | Produce Realisation Analysis | A | C | R | I | C |

Production of a Realisation Analysis is recommended regardless of whether a Benefit Workshop takes place or not. A Realisation Analysis is constructed right-to-left. It is best composed using 'Post-it' Pads and brown paper.

The aim is to identify any elements in one column that are not adequately enabled by one or more elements in the succeeding column so that any 'widow' or 'orphan' elements are eliminated – enabling is indicated by a line drawn between two boxes.

Integrity is proven when:

- Each strategic imperative is enabled by one or more objective

- Each objective is enabled by one or more benefit

- Each benefit is enabled by one or more change.

The enablers of each change and the components of the enablers are also identified.

Projects usually require changing the thinking and behaviour of impacted audiences as well as delivering 'things'. This may include customers as well as employees and suppliers. Make sure that full consideration is given to the changes, enablers and components required for this to happen, such as the changing of internal policies and procedures, supplier contracts, training, coaching, mentoring and communication.

Linkages must be true enabling links, for example, 'good documentation' does not automatically lead to 'improved productivity'. Someone has to use the documentation in a different way.

When agreed the composed information can be copied into a Realisation Analysis document and alphabetic and numeric cross-references added in place of the linkage lines.

| 3 | Agree Benefit Owners & measurement responsibility | R | C | A | I | C |

Benefit Owners need to make a personal, voluntary commitment to realise a benefit and not have it thrust upon them.

| 4 | Structure the benefits | R | C | A | I | C |

A Benefit Structure is a tool used to increase the explicitness of identified benefits. Each benefit is categorised on the Benefit Structure according to whether it arises from doing new things, doing things better or stopping doing things.

The degree of explicitness is expressed as:

- Financial – benefit realisation will be measured in real financial terms and has a direct impact on the profit & loss account or balance sheet

- Quantifiable difference – the before and after impact can be measured and will create a quantifiable difference

- Measureable – realisation of the benefit can be objectively measured

- Observable - realisation of the benefit can be subjectively assessed.

Benefits should be elevated until they reach their natural level and no further. Observable benefits should be discarded if they cannot be elevated to 'measurable'.

5	Analyse Benefit Owner commitment		R		A		I	

Commitment Analysis is a tool used to evaluate the commitment of Benefit Owners to realising benefits identified in the Benefit Plan.

> *A benefit to the organisation might seem like a disbenefit to a customer domain manager.*

A view can be taken of each Benefit Owner's actual and required level of commitment:

- Make it happen

- Help it happen

- Advocate

- Indifferent

- Unconvinced

- Uncooperative

- Hostile

If a Benefit Owner is displaying a lower or higher than required level of commitment, the perceived resistance can generally be determined by tactful discussion.

Identify where people are concerned about their ability to realise benefits and work with them to find ways to help them overcome the resistance.

This will mean understanding the Benefit Owner's challenges and personal objectives and why the benefits might conflict. Once the reason for the resistance is understood, the Project Sponsor and Project Leader can agree the appropriate action to gain commitment.

Inevitably, this will mean persuading the Benefit Owner to think and behave differently. The Communication Plan can be used to influence audiences.

6	Produce Benefit Plan		R		A	I		I

Populate the Benefit Plan with the information obtained. Only benefits that have an owner and are measurable are allowed.

Both the Cost Benefit Analysis and the Project Definition are likely to change as a result of Benefit Planning. If, as a result, the viability of the project has changed, the Project Sponsor should review the project with the Executive Sponsor before the end of High Level Planning.

Return to the Project Definition process at this point.

Benefit Workshop

A Benefit Workshop is a facilitated meeting attended by the Business Owner, Project Stakeholders and customer domain managers, the aim of which is to:

- Determine the dependencies between strategic imperatives, benefits, objectives and proposed changes
- Quantify the benefits
- Agree the ownership and realisation timetable and ownership of each benefit.

All workshop attendees should expect to take an active, participative role, supported and guided by the facilitator and co-facilitator.

Business Owner Role

The team relies upon the Business Owner to articulate the project vision, defend the objectives, and explain the key deliverables. Then, having listened to all challenges and viewpoints, make final judgements.

Benefit Owner Role

A Benefit Owner is a domain manager who accepts responsibility for realising a project benefit and who:

- Makes a personal commitment
- Plans the realisation of the benefit
- Negotiates the benefit amount and realisation date
- Acts to realise the benefit.

Customer domain managers and Project Stakeholders are the potential Benefit Owners.

Measurement Role

Finance and other domains within the organisation are empowered to alter business-as-usual budgets and performance targets to reflect the planned benefits. They will also have the capability to measure and report on benefit realisation.

Facilitation Role

The facilitation role is to inject energy and enthusiasm so that the whole exercise is completed successfully.

Success relies on the facilitator and co-facilitator each having the necessary competencies and business experience to grasp the fundamentals of the project in

---

the context in which it is being implemented. They also need to be familiar with using the Benefit Planning tools.

During the workshop the facilitator will:

- Extract views

- Question opinions in order to provoke debate and test the strength of arguments

- Challenge softness and imprecision

- Enforce precise wording

- Get empowered people to take responsibility for realising the benefits.

To perform their roles effectively, the facilitator and co-facilitator must earn the confidence, trust and respect of the team.

Organising the Benefit Workshop

A Benefit Workshop normally takes place over one full day. Plan to break every 2 hours with 30 minute gaps.

Before the Workshop

The facilitator and co-facilitator must carry out necessary preparatory work so that they have sufficient understanding to confidently practice the assertive style of facilitation needed. This includes carrying out research so as to appreciate industry issues. Preparatory work must be done at speed.

The facilitator should pre-meet with each workshop attendee to understand personal viewpoints and objectives, and build rapport. These meetings also provide a two-way opportunity to educate and inform.

Attendees will be asked to bring with them only what they can carry in their heads as there will be no opportunity to present. Persuasion is through listening, dialogue and debate.

During the Workshop

Workshop sessions need to fire in quick succession to maintain the necessary momentum. Persistence and continuity are required to see the process through to a successful conclusion.

Disputes are recorded in a 'Car Park'. This procedure allows the workshop to proceed at speed - giving people the opportunity to review issues after a cooling-off period, when each party may better understand the other point of view.

See Workshop facilitation Guidelines.

After the Workshop

It's the responsibility of the facilitator to consolidate and circulate the output from the Benefit Workshop.

It's unlikely that the output will be formed entirely right at the workshop. There will be 'blank spots' that need filling-in and areas that need clarification. The Project Leader can follow up on these afterwards.

Analysis & Consolidation Checklist

1	Does the project have sufficient customer domains to justify a Benefit Workshop or is it sufficient to generate the Benefit Plan informally?
2	Has the Benefit Workshop facilitator met and spoken with each workshop attendee before the Benefit Workshop?
3	Have the benefits been structured?
4	Has the workshop output been consolidated, fully populated and circulated to the attendees for final feedback?
5	Has a Benefit Plan been created and agreed by the Business Owner?
6	Does the Cost Benefit Analysis align with the Benefit Plan?
7	Does the Project Definition need revising?

Tips

- A Benefit Plan is needed for every project
- Benefit Workshops are expensive and not every project will need one.

Benefit Realisation

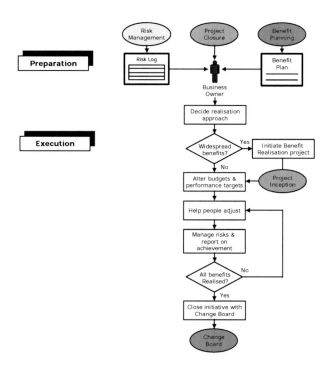

Figure 20: Benefit Realisation Process Map

Benefit Realisation is the process by which Executive Sponsors, Business Owners and Benefit Owners take full advantage of every opportunity to realise value in line with the Benefit Plan.

Benefits will have been planned and each Benefit Owner's commitment to delivery agreed and measurement responsibility assigned in Benefit Planning.

It's not just a matter of "Time's up – we've met the project objectives". Benefit realisation is the only measure of project success. It is triggered when a customer domain accepts a key deliverable. This may start during Project Delivery but will certainly continue beyond Project Closure.

The Business Owner is accountable to the Executive Sponsor for the realisation and measurement activities and management of open risks to benefit realisation - work that continues following Project Closure.

At all times, the Business Owner should be looking for Benefit Owners to realise the promised benefits and provide necessary evidence.

Wherever the line is drawn, the result will be that the planned benefits are either under or over estimated. The risks and opportunities associated with realisation must be actively managed.

The Executive Sponsor and Business Owner should always be asking the question "Are there any further benefits to be gained?"

Who does what?

- The Executive Sponsor should monitor benefit realisation from the Benefit Report, seek further benefit and measure business-as-usual performance against targets.

- The Business Owner should:

  - Maintain Benefit Owner commitment

  - Actively manage the risks to benefit realisation

  - Evaluate requested changes to the Benefit Plan

  - Resolve issues

  - Use the Benefit Report, to inform the Executive Sponsor and the Change Board of achievement.

- Benefit Owners should:

  - Maintain their personal commitment

  - Act to realise the benefit and help people adjust

  - Manage people's expectations

  - Evidence realisation.

- The people responsible for measuring benefit realisation contribute to preparation of the Benefit Report.

Preparation

Steps

		Executive Sponsor	Business Owner	Benefit Owner	Measurement responsibility	Change Board
R = Responsible						
A = Accountable						
C = Contribute						
I = Informed						
1	Decide realisation approach	R	A	C	C	I

The Business Owner will have the Benefit Plan and Risk Log.

The Business Owner should meet with the Benefit Owners and the people responsible for measuring benefit realisation to agree how the benefits will be realised and reported.

Together, they must decide where benefits will happen naturally through the business-as-usual processes or need to be driven out through continual improvement activity.

2	Widespread benefits?	A	I	R	I	I

If the benefits need to be realised across a number of domains which are outside the Business Owner's authority, it may be beneficial to create a benefit realisation project to help drive them out.

3	Alter business-as-usual budgets & performance targets	A	I	A	R	I

The Business Owner should work with the people empowered to change the organisation's budgets and performance targets to apply the quantities, measures and targets in the Benefit Plan.

Preparation Checklist

1	Does the Business Owner have a Benefit Plan and Risk Log?
2	Is there a plan for benefit realisation?
3	Is there a need for a benefit realisation project? If so, has it been initiated?
4	Have business-as-usual budgets and performance targets been changed?

Execution

Steps

		Executive Sponsor	Business Owner	Benefit Owner	Measurement responsibility	Change Board
	R = Responsible					
	A = Accountable					
	C = Contribute					
	I = Informed					
1	Help people adjust	A	A	R		

Some people will welcome change and adapt immediately. Others need more time to realise their potential.

Although audience focussed communication and training will have occurred during the course of the project, getting people to alter their thinking and behaviour is always a much greater challenge than changing 'things'.

After handover and acceptance a risk is that people will revert to their old unconscious ways of working. If this is allowed to happen, the anticipated benefits may not last or even materialise.

To prevent this from happening direct action might be needed like 'burning the physical and emotional bridges' which have sustained the old behaviours, so that people can see there is no way back. Invariably, this will mean aligning HR policies and procedures around performance improvement.

This can be coupled with effort from the Benefit Owners to help people adjust.

If people are struggling, they will be struggling either with the processes or behaviours in relation to their personal vision, goals and objectives. Support can be given in the form of coaching and mentoring:

- Coaching is a process where one person interacts with another in a particular context that results in improving the future for the other person. A coach will never advise or impose their solutions. The skills are easy to teach and once learnt, they can be used to help others.

- Mentoring uses a coaching attitude and process to allow someone to realise their potential, where the mentor has some experience or judgement about the topic. A mentor would normally guide and teach, drawing on their experience to lead the person towards a pre-determined goal or outcome.

When coaching or mentoring, it's important not to take responsibility away by telling someone 'what to do'. If you tell them what to do, they will probably not do it. This is because, generally, people do what they want not what they need.

Coaching and mentoring uses the pre-supposition that people have all the internal resources they need and there are no un-resourceful people only un-resourceful states.

Mindful of this, in day-to-day working, it's good practice when someone seeks direction to clarify the context and then ask the question "What do you think needs to be done?" Similarly, if they challenge what has been done, ask "So what's the alternative?"

If the response is satisfactory, then two further questions are needed:

- "What's stopping you?"
- "What do you need from me?"

If benefit realisation is dependent upon people altering their thinking and behaviours, consider the arrangements you might need to make for teaching coaching and mentoring skills.

2	Manage risks and report on achievement	I	R	C	C	I

It is inevitable that some benefits will take time to realise. The Executive Sponsor and Business Owner should:

- Monitor and review achievement with the Benefit Owner at agreed intervals
- Manage the risks to benefit realisation
- Seek the potential for further benefit.

Perseverance with the Benefit Plan, measurement responsibility and reporting using the Benefit Report through to the Change Board will yield the greatest positive results for the organisation.

If at any time benefits disappear or are reduced, a reassessment of the Benefit Plan should be undertaken in conjunction with the Change Board.

If an organisational change takes place, invalidating a benefit, a corresponding alteration to the Business Plan needs to be agreed by Executive Sponsor.

3	All benefits realised?	A	R	A	C	I

The process continues until targets are met.

4	Close initiative with Change Board	A	R	I	I	I

Benefit realisation ends when all planned benefits have been realised or exceeded.

Execution Checklist

1	Do people need help to adjust to the new business-as-usual environment?
2	Have the physical and emotional bridges back to the old culture been removed?
3	If needed, are arrangements for teaching coaching and mentoring skills in place?
4	Is benefit realisation being actively monitored and reviewed?
5	Are risks to benefit realisation being actively managed?
6	Is the difference being measured?
7	Is the realisation of benefits being reported to the Executive Sponsor and the Change Board?

Deliverable Management

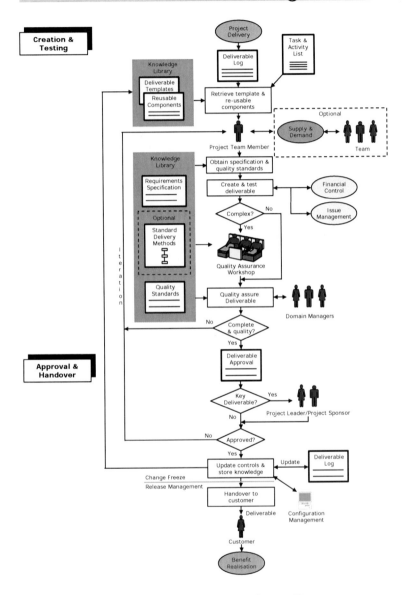

Figure 21: Deliverable Management Process Map

A deliverable is a change which contributes towards at least one objective, and hence the realisation of benefit, created by one domain and formally accepted by another domain.

If the project is to be successful, every deliverable must be produced 'fit-for-purpose', on time and within budget.

Deliverable Management is the process by which deliverables are created, tested and operationally proven so that quality is assured.

> *Quality deliverables don't 'just happen' - the Project Leader should insist that sufficient activities and iterations are built in to the **Task & Activity List** to guarantee success.*

Creation & Testing

Steps

		Project Sponsor	Domain Manager	Project Team Member	Project Leader	Project Partner	BAU Team
	R = Responsible A = Accountable C = Contribute I = Informed						
1	Retrieve template & reusable components		A	R	A	A	C

Before commencing the creation of a deliverable, the Project Team Member should check the organisation's Knowledge Library to see if a similar deliverable has been previously created that can be re-used as a template or if there are re-usable components available form a previous project.

| 2 | Obtain specification & quality standards | | A | R | A | A | C |

Obtain the Requirements Specification, which describes the functionality, usability and acceptability of the deliverable, and the relevant quality standards so that its quality can be objectively assessed. If applicable, use the associated development method to guide efficient creation of the deliverable,

> *A quality standard is the specific parameters or definitions by which the quality of a deliverable can be assessed:*
>
> - *For compliance with statutory, regulatory, legal or industry standards*
> - *To mitigate risk*
> - *To attain accreditation*

3	Create & test the deliverable		A	R	A	A	C

The work of creating a deliverable is the responsibility of a named Project Team Member and done by that person or by a team within the Project Team Member's business-as-usual domain.

If creation of the deliverable requires the spending of money, check with the Project Leader that this expenditure is covered by the project budget and has been properly authorised, before making any commitments.

This work should include testing of every component and feature of the deliverable, if appropriate, as well as of the complete deliverable, under version control.

> ## The customer perceives a quality deliverable as one that is:
>
> - ■ *Fit for its intended purpose*
> - ■ *Defect free within agreed tolerances*
> - ■ *Value for money*

The iterations needed to create a quality deliverable are estimated during Detailed Planning. If this is insufficient then there is an issue to be resolved.

Creation and testing of some deliverables might take a fixed length of time, regardless of the amount of effort applied – a 'natural duration'. Don't be tempted to compromise quality by taking short cuts. Manage the expectations of your customer when deliverable creation and testing has a natural duration.

4	Quality assure deliverable		R	C	A	A	

A deliverable is not complete until it has been 'signed-off' by the relevant supplier and customer domain managers.

If the deliverable is complex, or if two or more domain mangers have different opinions, the Project Leader should organise a Quality Assurance Workshop.

Quality Assurance Workshop

The quality assurance of a complex deliverable may require a Quality Assurance Workshop - a facilitated meeting of relevant individuals to review a deliverable against its specification and quality standards, and unanimously agree its deficiencies in time for them to be corrected.

Creation & Testing Checklist

1	Has a similar deliverable been created previously or does a template exist in the Knowledge Library?
2	Are there re-usable components in the Knowledge Library that can be used to save time and money?
3	Does the deliverable have a specification, relevant quality standards and an associated development method?
4	Can the deliverable be created and tested within the planned number of iterations?
5	Has the deliverable been quality assured and agreed?

Approval & Handover

Steps

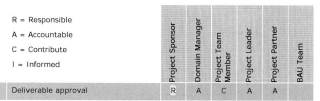

		Project Sponsor	Domain Manager	Project Team Member	Project Leader	Project Partner	BAU Team
1	Deliverable approval	R	A	C	A	A	

If accepted each supplier domain representative will need to sign the Deliverable Approval. If it is a key deliverable, the Project Leader and Project Sponsor will also need to approve it before delivery to the customer. If rejected, return to Creation & Testing.

		Project Sponsor	Domain Manager	Project Team Member	Project Leader	Project Partner	BAU Team
2	Update controls and store knowledge	I	I	I	R	A	

The Project Leader flags each approved deliverable as complete in the Deliverable Log. Each completed deliverable is then 'baselined' to a version number and thereafter subject to change control. If the deliverable is part of a complex entity, such as, an IT application implementation might be controlled through Configuration Management system operated by the system owner.

> **Configuration Management is a tool used by the owner of a complex system to control implementation and change so that an audit trail is maintained and, in the event of system failure a controlled recovery can take place with minimal disruption to business continuity.**

Component deliverables may not be handed over to the customer until all the deliverables making up the higher-order deliverable are assembled. These deliverables may be placed under a change freeze until they are all complete.

If the deliverable can be used as a template or contains components that could be re-used on a future project, the template and components should be created by the Project Team Member and stored in the Knowledge Library.

		Project Sponsor	Domain Manager	Project Team Member	Project Leader	Project Partner	BAU Team
3	Handover to customer	A	A	A	R	A	C

Handover and acceptance of the deliverable by the customer is confirmed using the Deliverable Approval.

Deliverables impacting a complex operating environment should be applied through 'release management'. See - Working with a Development Method.

After handover the deliverable becomes the property of a customer domain and the customer can trigger benefit realisation activities.

Approval & Handover Checklist

1	Has the Deliverable Approval been signed by supplier and customer domain managers, and the Deliverable Log updated?
2	Has the Deliverable Log been updated?

3	Has the deliverable been 'baselined' to a version number?
4	Have deliverables, which can be used as templates been added to the Knowledge Library?
5	Have components, which can be re-used on a future project, been added to the Knowledge Library?
6	Does the deliverable need to be 'frozen' to change and stored?
7	Does Configuration Management apply to the operating environment you are impacting?
8	Is handover best managed through release management?
9	Has the customer prepared themselves for the handover and acceptance?
10	Has the deliverable been handed over to and accepted by the customer?

Tips

- Always quality assure to specification and quality standards - quality itself is not a variable

- If you present a formal Deliverable Approval document for signature, people are more likely to take quality assurance seriously

- Where contention exists, facilitate a Quality Assurance Workshop - ensure that the final owner of the deliverable is a participant

- Use cost and manpower contingency to contend with adverse outcomes of risks, and then only with Project Sponsor approval

- Don't forget version control!

Issue Management

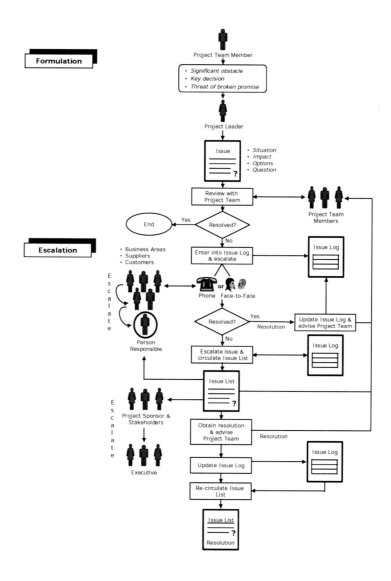

Figure 22: Issue Management Process Map

An issue is an unexpected circumstance or refuted assumption that will cause slippage to a current or imminent event unless it can be resolved.

It might be a significant obstacle, a key decision or the threat of a broken promise.

Issue Management is the process by which an identified issue is recorded and escalated to a level at which it can be resolved. When resolved it may create new issues or risks.

> **An issue is not a disaster, simply an obstacle to be removed.**

The Project Leader must be alerted to an issue as soon as it is recognised. This should be made clear to everyone involved.

Issue Management is a simple process, demanding strong resolve and good interpersonal communication skills. It requires the Project Leader to be empowered by the Project Sponsor and the Executive Sponsor to communicate issues using the Issue List.

Formulation

Issues need not be confrontational or stressful if they are worded in a factual, accurate, precise, concise, impersonal and non-judgemental manner.

They are best structured in four parts:

- Situation – a description of the frustration
- Impact – the consequence of the situation on benefits, quality, cost, manpower and time
- Options – acceptable ways of resolving the issue
- Question – essentially, what is the resolution?

Steps

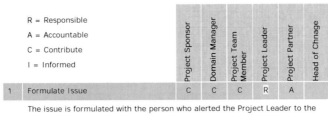

		Project Sponsor	Domain Manager	Project Team Member	Project Leader	Project Partner	Head of Chnage
1	Formulate Issue	C	C	C	R	A	

The issue is formulated with the person who alerted the Project Leader to the issue.

2	Review with Project Team			C	R	A	

Issues can impact more than one domain, if so it is best formulated with the Project Team Members of all these domains. There is a fair chance that the clarity this brings will immediately find an acceptable resolution.

R = Responsible
A = Accountable
C = Contribute
I = Informed

Escalation

> **The Project Leader must take personal ownership of each issue and retain responsibility through escalation until a satisfactory resolution is obtained.**

Steps

		Project Sponsor	Domain Manager	Project Team Member	Project Leader	Project Partner	Head of Chnage
	R = Responsible A = Accountable C = Contribute I = Informed						
1	Enter into Issue Log and escalate				R	A	

Only include genuine issues in the Issue Log. If an issue evaporates before it is resolved, eject it from the Issue Log. If the issue is formulated and escalated the resolution must be logged so as to form the audit trail.

Once formulated, the issue is first escalated informally. It can be communicated by email but face-to face communication is the preferred way to quickly establish the person responsible, and obtain a resolution.

At each level ask:

"Are you empowered to answer the question?"

"Yes" – "Great, what is the answer?"

"No" – "Can you indicate the person who is and will you lend your support?"

The person may suggest rewording the issue to sharpen it up.

Continue to escalate the issue until the person empowered to resolve it is identified. When escalating, never by-pass a layer of management.

		Project Sponsor	Domain Manager	Project Team Member	Project Leader	Project Partner	Head of Chnage
2	Resolved?	I	I	I	R	A	

Well-drafted contracts and service agreements will place the challenge of issue resolution with the supplier responsible.

An ideal resolution does not cause any target date or deadline to be missed and has no adverse impact on project cost, manpower or benefits. However, if slippage is threatened, agree appropriate action with the project team and alert the Project Sponsor to the risk, using the Risk Management process.

		Project Sponsor	Domain Manager	Project Team Member	Project Leader	Project Partner	Head of Chnage
3	Add issue to Issue List	I	I	I	R	A	I

An issue is escalated to the Issue List if its resolution is being blocked, evaded or unduly delayed by indecision so threatening to cause slippage. Before putting it on the Issue List, if time allows, apply a 'three chance' guideline:

- Give the person a chance to comply

- Give the person a second chance to comply

- Escalate the intransigence as an issue on the Issue List.

Key decisions are always shown on the Issue Log as being resolved the same day, unless intransigence is encountered, in which case the Issue List should be employed.

Circulation of the Issue List to the Project Sponsor and Project Stakeholders and Change Board will draw attention to the impact of issues on project success and usually results in a rapid resolution.

		I	I	I	R	A	I
4	Obtain resolution, advise Project Team Members	I	I	I	R	A	I

No issue should remain unresolved for more than one week and depending on the stage a project has reached, 'same day issue resolution' may be necessary. However the issue is resolved, the resolution must be communicated to the Project Team Members impacted.

5	Update Issue Log and re-circulate the Issue List	I	I	I	R	A	I

A resolved issue is closed and the audit trail completed by updating the Issue Log. If the Issue List was used, it should be re-circulated showing the resolution, and then the issue can be removed.

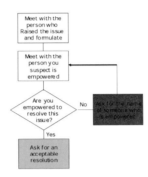

Figure 23: Escalation

Escalation Checklist

1	Did you agree with the Project Sponsor the use and circulation of the Issue List during shaping of the project?
2	Are all issues resolved? If so, have you circulated an Issue List stating 'There are no issues'?

Tips

- Don't clutter the Issue Log with trivia which is easily resolved
- Formulate options, not problems - and ask a question
- Unattended issues cause projects to fail – expedite resolutions and circulate the Issue List weekly
- Circulate the Issue List to the Executive Sponsor, Project Sponsor and Project Stakeholders to give it power
- If there are no issues, circulate an Issue List stating 'There are no issues'
- Restate issues on the Issue List until resolved

Risk Management

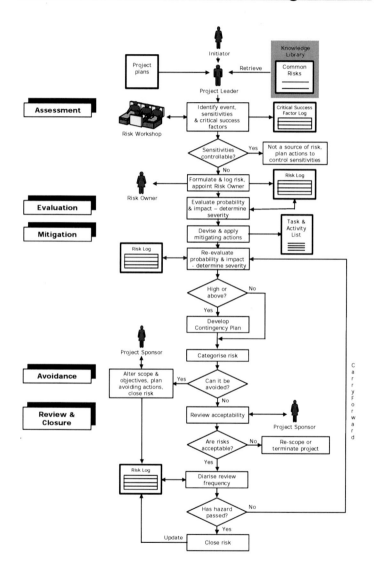

Figure 24: Risk Management Process Map

A risk is the adverse outcome of a future event that is subject to chance and which threatens achievement of objectives, and realisation of benefits.

> **Risks cannot be controlled – only managed.**

Projects are made up of events, which are planned in stages, phases, tasks and activities, producing deliverables that enable financial and non-financial benefits.

> **An event is something that takes you towards the achievement of objectives and realisation of benefits.**

Risk Management is the process of making the risks inherent in a project explicit, and increasing the likelihood of success by:

- Assessing the risks to the outcome of the project
- Evaluating the probability and impact
- Determining mitigating actions
- Making contingency plans for high and unacceptable risks
- Seeking ways of avoiding risks
- Monitoring and re-assessing risks at agreed intervals.

It is a 'dip in-and-out' process used throughout the project – used not just a once at the beginning but whenever a risk is identified or even suspected.

Risks stem from the 'sensitivities' surrounding an event with the potential to impact project success.

> **A sensitivity is a factor to which the outcome of an event is sensitive - the factor may be:**
>
> - **Controllable - in which case the work to control it must be in the project plan**
>
> - **Uncontrollable - in which case it is a source of risk to project delivery and the chance of lower or higher benefit.**

Sources of sensitivity include:

- Anticipated occurrences stemming from the context of the event
- Decisions yet to be made which are covered by assumptions
- Changes to the objectives or additions to the scope of the project.

Risk Workshop

A Risk Workshop is a facilitated meeting of relevant subject matter experts and relevant domain managers to determine the severity of risks associated with an event within a project, and to generate appropriate mitigating actions and contingency plans.

A Risk Workshop is usually the best forum for conducting the risk management process. They can be held at any time - at least one Risk Workshop should be held.

Assessment

Assessment is the process of determining exposure of an event to chance so that the risk of an adverse outcome can be determined and managed.

Steps

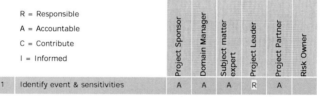

		Project Sponsor	Domain Manager	Subject matter expert	Project Leader	Project Partner	Risk Owner
	R = Responsible						
	A = Accountable						
	C = Contribute						
	I = Informed						
1	Identify event & sensitivities	A	A	A	R	A	

In preparation for assessment, the Project Leader needs to review common risks, extract sensitivities from the Bid and identify the major events in the project.

Events are analysed to determine sensitivities in relation to the objectives and scope, and assumptions made about the project. Everyone involved in the workshop must help to identify possible sensitivities.

2	Are the sensitivities controllable?		C	C	R	A	C

If the sensitivities surrounding an event are controllable, then the work to control them must be in the project plan. If a sensitivity is uncontrollable it is a source of risk. The Project Leader should seek expert opinion before deciding.

Decide the project's critical success factors in the light of the sensitivities and agree with the Project Sponsor to alter them if necessary. Include them on the Critical Success Factor Log, if this is used, or change the Project Definition.

3	Formulate risk & appoint a Risk Owner		A	A	A	A	R

Define the outcome that could occur if at least one, uncontrollable sensitivity is adverse. State the risk in the form: 'The risk is that...'

Consider the project objectives and benefits that would be in jeopardy if this adverse outcome occurred.

One subject matter expert should be appointed 'Risk Owner'. The Risk Owner, having listened to the different points of view, is responsible for taking the final decision in respect of risk severity, agreeing mitigating actions, monitoring the risk and recommending use of the contingency plan.

Following the workshop the Project Leader should record the outcomes on the Risk Log.

Assessment Checklist

1	Is it clear to everyone involved in the project that they must alert you to all possible sensitivities and risks in relation to planned events?
2	Have you obtained common risks from the Knowledge Library and extracted the sensitivities surrounding the benefit realisation events from the Bid?
3	Have the risks been formulated in relation to the uncontrollable sensitivities surrounding events and added to the Risk Log?

Evaluation

Evaluation is the process of quantifying risk probability and impact so that it can be managed in relation to its severity. All risks should be evaluated for probability and impact, even those you aim to avoid.

Evaluating Probability

A value judgement is made to rate probability in terms of low, medium or high:

Low	Medium	High
The chance is not zero but it is more likely not to occur than occur	It is about as likely to occur as not to occur	It is much more likely to occur than not to occur

Evaluating Impact

A value judgement is then made to rate overall impact in terms of small, moderate or large. The impact of an adverse outcome is 'slippage'. Slippage can impact four factors – quality, time, resources and benefits. Choose the factor for which the impact is highest.

	Small	Moderate	Large
Quality	A key deliverable has minor deficiencies	A key deliverable requires many workarounds	A key deliverable is unfit for purpose
Time	Causing minor delay to project delivery	Causing significant delay to project delivery	Causing a major delay to project delivery
Resources	Minor increase in total project cost or manpower: up to 10%	Significant increase to total project cost or manpower: 11-25%	Major increase to total project cost or manpower: >26%
Benefits	Loss of some benefits: up to 25%	Significant loss of benefits: 26-50%	Major loss of benefits: 51-100%

Determining Severity

Risk severity can be determined using the following table.

Probability		x	Impact		=	Severity
Low	1		Small	2	2,3	Low
Medium	2		Moderate	3	4	Medium
High	4		Large	4	6,8	High
					12,16	Unacceptable

Mitigation

Steps

R = Responsible
A = Accountable
C = Contribute
I = Informed

		Project Sponsor	Domain Manager	Subject matter expert	Project Leader	Project Partner	Risk Owner
1	Devise & apply mitigating actions	C	C	A	A		R

A mitigating action is work that could be done before or during an event to reduce the probability or lessen the impact. The aim is to identify deliverables or work that can be added to the project so that there is less chance of the adverse outcome occurring or, if it does, its impact is reduced. Mitigating actions are likely to cost money, use manpower and take time.

2	Re-evaluate probability and impact, and re-determine severity	C	C	A	A		R

Evaluation of the impact and probability should be repeated on the assumption that the mitigating actions have been put in place. If a risk remains at 'unacceptable' severity then the Project Sponsor should be alerted and asked to consider re-scoping the objectives or even terminating the project if the subsequent loss of benefits is too great.

3	Develop contingency plans	C	C	A	A		R

A Contingency Plan is a scheme planned in detail for use in the event of, and to recover from, the adverse outcome of a specific risk.

Contingency plans are work that will be done should the adverse outcome occur, that recover at least some of the loss of objective or enable the project to be terminated cleanly.

A Contingency Plan will cost money, use manpower and take time. The cost will only be incurred if the adverse outcome occurs – and then only with the approval of the Project Sponsor.

Contingency plans are required for risks that remain of high or unacceptable severity and optional for risks of low or medium severity.

4	Categorise risk	C	C	R	A		C

You should now have sufficient understanding to decide the risk type. There are possible four risk types. Three of these, strategic, operational and external relate to the benefit realisation event which is the responsibility of the Business Owner.

Risk Type	Threatening
Strategic	The organisation's strategy and business plan in relation to its target market, where the sensitivities emanate largely from assumptions
Operational	The business-as-usual operations of the organisation, where the sensitivities emanate largely from hazards
External	Viability of the project's business case, in respect of political, economic, social, technological, legal or environmental threats, where the sensitivities emanate largely from assumptions
Delivery	Delivery of the project within agreed targets, where the sensitivities emanate from planned events and assumptions

Mitigation Checklist

1	Have mitigating actions and deliverables, if appropriate, been devised and have they been 'costed'?
2	Have activities relating to mitigating actions, been included in the Task & Activity List and deliverables added to the Deliverable Log?
3	Have all risks been re-evaluated, assuming mitigating actions and deliverables are in place?
4	Do any unacceptable risks remain and has the Project Sponsor been alerted?
5	Has the Risk Log been updated?
6	Have Contingency Plans, if appropriate, been devised and costed, and are these costs covered by the contingency allowance?
7	Has the risk type been confirmed?

Avoidance

Steps

R = Responsible
A = Accountable
C = Contribute
I = Informed

		Project Sponsor	Domain Manager	Project Team Member	Project Leader	Project Partner	Risk Owner
1	Can it be avoided?	C	C	C	R	A	C

If a risk is to be avoided, then some aspects of the project scope and objectives probably have to alter. And, more often than not, the costs, manpower, target date for completion or the benefits will change.

Transferring the risk to an external supplier who is better able to mitigate the risk and absorb the impact might be a mitigating action but is not a means of avoiding the risk. However, the risk to the project will still remain and should not be overlooked. Reasoned evaluation identifies what might be transferable.

2	Review acceptability	R	I	I	A	A	

The Project Sponsor may wish to compare the impact of carrying the risk with the impact of avoiding the risk. If the sponsor decides against avoiding the risk, the Project Leader should go back to Mitigation.

3	Implement avoidance actions	A	A	R	A	C

The Project Leader must amend all aspects of the project impacted by the avoidance action – this may include the Bid, the Project Definition, the Benefit Plan, and all planning and control documents. Expert opinion may be required.

4	Mark as closed on Risk Log	I	I	I	R	A	

Avoided risks are closed and no longer subject to a Risk Management process.

Avoidance Checklist

1	Have all aspects of the project scope and objectives been considered before deciding to avoid it?
2	If a risk is to be avoided, have changes to the project scope and objectives been made been made?
3	Have all other aspects of the project documentation been changed?
4	Have all avoided risks been marked as closed on the Risk Log?

Review & Closure

Steps

R = Responsible
A = Accountable
C = Contribute
I = Informed

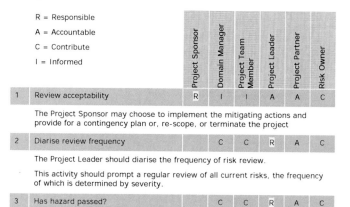

		Project Sponsor	Domain Manager	Project Team Member	Project Leader	Project Partner	Risk Owner
1	Review acceptability	R	I	I	A	A	C

The Project Sponsor may choose to implement the mitigating actions and provide for a contingency plan or, re-scope, or terminate the project

2	Diarise review frequency		C	C	R	A	C

The Project Leader should diarise the frequency of risk review.

This activity should prompt a regular review of all current risks, the frequency of which is determined by severity.

3	Has hazard passed?		C	C	R	A	C

A risk must be monitored until all chance of an adverse outcome has passed. When the hazard has passed close the risk.

Risks to benefit realisation will remain open after Project Closure and become the responsibility of the Business Owner.

Contingency Allowance

> *A judgement is made after all known risks have been assessed, mitigated, and contingency plans produced – this is used to agree a realistic contingency allowance.*

When the cost of the contingency plans is known the overall exposure to delivery risk can be assessed and converted into a percentage contingency allowance.

Review all delivery risks and contingency plans with the Project Sponsor and negotiate a 'reasonable' contingency allowance.

Using the table below as a guide, a qualitative judgement can be made and a reasoned contingency allowance determined.

Exposure to delivery risk	Suggested Contingency Allowance
Minimal	Nil
Low	10%
Moderate	25%
High	40%
Very high	>40%

The percentage contingency allowance is added to the Manpower Estimate the Cost Estimate, and to the Bid for full funding.

Business Risk

The contingency allowance when added to the 'chance of lower financial benefit' makes up the 'business risk'. This is shown on the Bid document Investment Appraisal.

The Project Sponsor needs to be aware that if the cost of the contingency plans is very high, the organisation may be gambling the whole project investment or even the organisation itself. This information needs to be shared with the Executive Sponsor and Change Board.

Use of Contingency

The contingency allowance may only be used against an identified risk, and only with the permission of the Project Sponsor.

Tips

- Take pains to identify all possible sensitivities in relation to events – it's the risk you don't identify that will have the adverse outcome

- During High Level Planning, when consulting with subject matter experts, ask "What are the event sensitivities?"

- A change to specification and scope is a common risk that has a significant impact upon project success - either set aside sufficient contingency to mitigate for this or avoid the risk by adopting a 'no change' policy

- Don't consider 'silly' risks – like an asteroid hitting the earth!

- Remember, risks cannot be controlled - only managed - and an adverse outcome may not happen

- If an adverse outcome does occur, feel good that you planned and provided for it.

Change Control

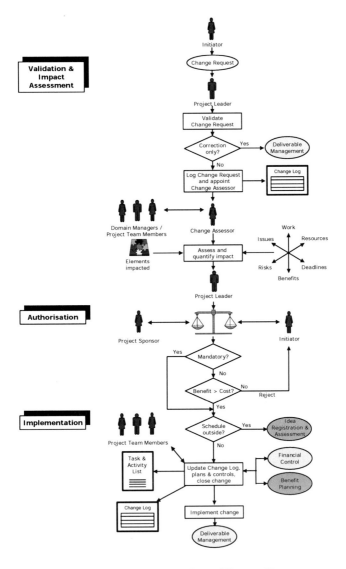

Figure 25: Change Control Process Map

         © Verdandi Limited 1984-2010

A change request is a necessary or wished-for modification to any aspect of a project - it is inevitable that people will request changes as the project proceeds, and have apparently good reasons for changing, the objectives, scope, deliverables, specifications, quality standards, targets, deadlines – the list is endless.

Change Control is the process by which requests for change to any aspect of a project are validated, assessed, rejected or authorised, implemented or deferred.

> *If change requests aren't controlled the rate of change will exceed the rate of progress, project costs will rise, the project will be late and the benefits will decline.*

Guidelines for applying the process are:

- Documents and deliverables under development are not subject to Change Control

- Other documents and deliverables may be 'baselined' to a version number – they can only be changed through Change Control

- Yet others may be frozen – they can't be changed at all, at least for a period of time.

The Project Leader must take pains to identify and prevent changes being made 'on the fly' - people must be stopped from circumventing the process by using, if necessary, the risk and issue management processes.

Validation & Impact Assessment

Steps

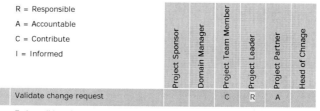

		Project Sponsor	Domain Manager	Project Team Member	Project Leader	Project Partner	Head of Chnage
R = Responsible							
A = Accountable							
C = Contribute							
I = Informed							
1	Validate change request			C	R	A	

To be valid, a change request must relate to an already baselined document or deliverable. The Project Leader must check that a change request is valid before proceeding.

If a mistake has been made, perhaps by someone incorrectly 'signing-off' a document or deliverable, the correction is more appropriately dealt with using the Deliverable Management processes.

2	Log change request and appoint change assessor	C	C	A	R	A	

Change requests must be recorded in the Change Log.

The assessor is generally the Project Team Member of the domain creating the document or deliverable. In some case, it may be appropriate to appoint a subject matter expert from the impacted domain to assess the change request.

If the change request is large, then several assessors may be needed.

3	Assess and quantify impact	C	C	C	R	A	

The appointed assessor must determine what work will be affected if the change request is approved - including:

- The work already done or needing to be re-done

- The resources – money and manpower – required to do the work

- The deadlines by which the work must be done

- The Benefit Plan

- The business risk, supported by details of the existing risks, as well as newly identified risks

- Any issues.

The Project Leader must check that the assessor has done a quality job.

Assessing & Quantifying Impact

The assessor of the change agrees the consequences of approving the change request by agreeing with relevant domain managers and Project Team Members that:

- Some work might not need to be done

- Other work must be:

  - Undone – note that some work, like demolition, may be irreversible

  - Done again in a different way

  - Done in addition.

The assessor can determine the impact on the Benefit Plan, in agreement with the relevant Benefit Owners.

The assessment and quantification of impact should be documented and 'signed-off' – the Change Log contains only a summary.

By agreeing estimates and target dates for the revised work, the assessor can easily determine the resources required.

If these new target dates mean that a deadline cannot be achieved, there is an issue to be resolved if the change request is approved.

The assessor can determine the impact on risk by identifying if the sensitivities have altered and if any are uncontrollable.

Authorisation

Steps

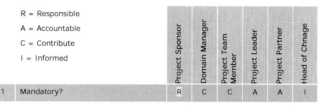

		Project Sponsor	Domain Manager	Project Team Member	Project Leader	Project Partner	Head of Chnage
	R = Responsible A = Accountable C = Contribute I = Informed						
1	Mandatory?	R	C	C	A	A	I

The approval of a change request may be mandatory – brought about by a change to a legal, regulatory, statutory or group holding company requirement. The approval of such a change may alter the Cost Benefit Analysis to the extent that the Bid must be re-submitted to the Change Board.

2	Benefit > Cost?	R	C	C	A	A	I

The Project Sponsor may have empowered the Project Leader to make small, change request decisions. For the most part, the Project Sponsor must make the decision. The decision may be to:

- Reject the change – in which case the Project Leader must inform those affected and close the change request

- Defer to some later date – perhaps as a new initiative - in which case the Project Leader must inform those affected and close the change request.

- Approve its immediate implementation.

Implementation

Steps

		Project Sponsor	Domain Manager	Project Team Member	Project Leader	Project Partner	Head of Chnage
	R = Responsible A = Accountable C = Contribute I = Informed						
1	Update documents	I	I	I	R	A	I

For a change request approved for immediate implementation, the Project Leader must update all relevant planning and control documents, including the Bid – and inform those affected.

2	Close change request	I	I	I	R	A	I

Once the Project Leader has taken all necessary actions, the Change Log can be updated.

3	Implement change	I	I	I	R	A	I

Changes are applied through Deliverable Management. Implementation of changes should always involve version control – see Techniques.

Change Control Checklist

1	Is the Change Log up to date?
2	Is the appointed change assessor fit-for-purpose?
3	Do you have a quality assessment and quantification of the requested change?
4	Have all change requests been processed through assessment and quantification to a final decision?
5	Have you amended the Cost Benefit Analysis and Bid, if appropriate?
6	Have you applied the authorised changes through Deliverable Management?

Tips

- Discuss the need for strict Change Control with the Project Sponsor whilst agreeing the project shape

- Evaluate all valid change requests

- Remember, there's no such thing as a change request that can be implemented for 'free'

- You will need to update planning and control documents whenever a change request is approved - if an objective, key deliverable, deadline, or element of scope is changed you will need to update the Project Definition; the Cost Benefit Analysis must be updated for each approved change request.

Supplier Engagement

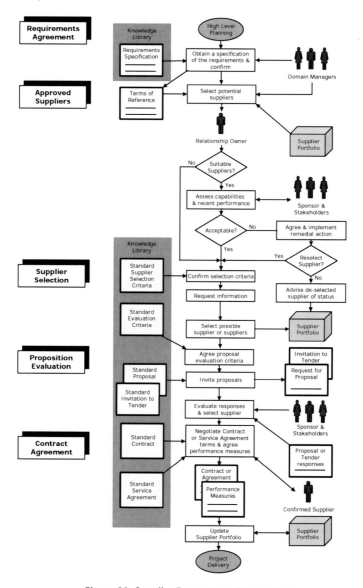

Figure 26: Supplier Engagement Process Map

Supplier Engagement is the process by which suppliers are selected, evaluated and formally appointed.

> **Inadequate specifications and weak supplier contracts are root causes of delivery disputes, overspending, missed deadlines and customer disappointment.**

Each organisation has its own policies and processes for procuring products and services from external suppliers appropriate to the nature of its business – this process can be used in conjunction.

The process begins as soon as the key deliverables are known and, if alternative solutions are being considered, before the preferred alternative is decided – see Techniques: Working with a Development Method.

Internal suppliers are usually appointed informally – to avert risks, the rigour of applying this process is worthy of consideration but using a service agreement instead of a contract.

Requirements Agreement

Steps

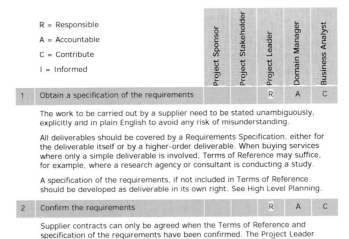

		Project Sponsor	Project Stakeholder	Project Leader	Domain Manager	Business Analyst
	R = Responsible A = Accountable C = Contribute I = Informed					
1	Obtain a specification of the requirements			R	A	C

The work to be carried out by a supplier need to be stated unambiguously, explicitly and in plain English to avoid any risk of misunderstanding.

All deliverables should be covered by a Requirements Specification, either for the deliverable itself or by a higher-order deliverable. When buying services where only a simple deliverable is involved, Terms of Reference may suffice, for example, where a research agency or consultant is conducting a study.

A specification of the requirements, if not included in Terms of Reference should be developed as deliverable in its own right. See High Level Planning.

2	Confirm the requirements			R	A	C

Supplier contracts can only be agreed when the Terms of Reference and specification of the requirements have been confirmed. The Project Leader should facilitate agreement with relevant domain mangers.

Requirements Agreement Checklist

1	Are Terms of Reference needed and are they fit for intended purpose?
2	Does an agreed specification of the deliverable or key deliverable exist - has it been signed-off by the owner?

Approved Suppliers

Steps

		Project Sponsor	Project Stakeholder	Project Leader	Domain Manager	Relationship Owner
R = Responsible A = Accountable C = Contribute I = Informed						
1	Select potential suppliers	I	I	I	R	A

One or more suppliers should be selected from the organisation's 'approved supplier list'.

Approved supplier means that a supplier that has already gone through and meets the organisation's supplier acceptance criteria, terms, and conditions of business. It is not intended as a barrier to exclude suppliers with different or innovative products and services.

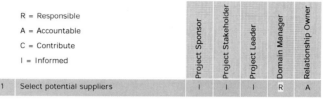

If something goes wrong as a consequence of a project, how suppliers were engaged and managed comes under scrutiny.

Unless the Project Leader or Project Partner has supplier selection expertise and authority, this work should be delegated to an empowered domain manager from the organisation.

2	Assess capabilities and recent performance			I	R	A

Customer domain managers should review each selected supplier's capabilities to ensure that in principle, they have recent and relevant experience and will be able to cope with the work.

3	Agree and implement remedial action			I	I	R

Based on previous experiences,supported by relevant Supplier Reviews, it may be necessary to agree remedial action before a supplier can be nominated for selection. A decision needs to be taken by the relationship owner as to whether to re-select the supplier.

4	Advise de-selected suppliers of status			I	I	R

Each supplier needs to be advised of their status by the relationship owner.

Any changes to supplier status or information should be included in the Supplier Portfolio.

Approved Suppliers Checklist

1	Can the supplier cope with the agreed requirements?
2	Have you obtained firm evidence of capability and a track record?
3	Is remedial action needed on the part of the supplier?
4	Can the supplier evidence that remedial action has taken place?
5	Should the supplier be put forward for selection?

Supplier Selection

Steps

		Project Sponsor	Project Stakeholder	Project Leader	Domain Manager	Relationship Owner
R = Responsible						
A = Accountable						
C = Contribute						
I = Informed						
1	Confirm selection criteria	I	I	I	R	A

The aim of this step is to allow the realistic contenders that are suited to the organisation to be identified so that either one supplier is selected or a short list of possible suppliers produced.

Care in selecting suppliers before awarding a contract or service agreement reduces the risk of issues surfacing during delivery - this has significant advantages to both the customer and the ultimate supplier.

If standard selection criteria exist in the Knowledge Library, then these should be reviewed and agreed then used. Otherwise, devise selection criteria – advice should be sought from the procurement function.

2	Request information			C	R	A

Identify and act upon the need for a mutual non-disclosure agreement.

Protect the confidentiality of customer and supplier intellectual property with appropriate non-disclosure agreements, signed by an authorised signatory of each organisation and all people working on the initiative.

If there is no suitable approved supplier or if additional new suppliers are to be considered then a Request for Information should be issued that includes:

- A statement of the information needed, including a request for a copy of the suppliers' terms of business

- A brief description of the requirement so that the supplier can assess the commercial opportunity

- A description of the intended selection process and selection criteria.

Interested suppliers should be asked to respond by an agreed deadline.

3	Select supplier or possible suppliers	C	C	C	R	A

Assess the supplier responses against the selection criteria.

Confirm with the legal function that the supplier's terms of business are fair, reasonable and in plain English. Insist on changes and caveats if they are not fair

Select one or two possible suppliers or, if it is a major piece of work, create a shortlist of possible suppliers. Inform each supplier of the outcome, giving deselected suppliers specific reasons for de-selection.

Terms of Business

It is important to clarify and confirm a supplier's terms of business before commencing any work. Considerations include:

Rates and conditions of working

- Rates, fees, prices and discount structures - this may be at no charge if it is an internal supplier where no cross-charging takes place
- Inclusions and exclusions, for example, tools, equipment, work space, accommodation, travel costs, expenses, taxes;
- Licence fees
- Expenses
- Local taxes
- Payment terms, including:
  - Fixed price or time and materials
  - Payment in arrears or pre-pay and call-off
  - Stage payment plan (% of work complete)
- Governing Law

Intellectual Property

Ownership of intellectual property and protection of rights should be clear and if part of the requirements, covered by an appropriate agreement.

Expenses

The policy for external suppliers should be consistent with that of internal suppliers.

Supplier Selection Checklist

1	Have the supplier selection criteria been agreed?
2	Is a mutual non-disclosure agreement needed?
3	Has one supplier been selected or is there a shortlist of possible suppliers?
4	Have successful and unsuccessful suppliers been informed.

Proposal Evaluation

A proposal is a supplier's response to a customer's specified requirement, setting out:

- Background, supplier overview and customer specified requirement
- The features, advantages and benefits of their products and services
- The supplier's capabilities and ability to meet the customer's specific requirements
- An estimate or quotation

> *An estimate is logically determined but non-binding.*
>
> *A quotation is a firm estimate from a supplier that is legally binding, within reasonable margins of error, typically 10%.*

- An implementation schedule.

Steps

		Project Sponsor	Project Stakeholder	Project Leader	Domain Manager	Relationship Owner
R = Responsible						
A = Accountable						
C = Contribute						
I = Informed						
1	Agree proposal evaluation criteria	C	C	C	R	A

To prevent evaluation becoming a 'beauty parade', it is important to define and agree in advance the criteria that will be used in the assessment. If standard evaluation criteria exist within the organisation, they should be retrieved from the Knowledge Library. If not, evaluation criteria will need to be devised. The criteria should be agreed by the Project Sponsor and Project Stakeholders.

		Project Sponsor	Project Stakeholder	Project Leader	Domain Manager	Relationship Owner
2	Invite proposals			C	R	A

There are two ways to elicit supplier proposals - a Request for Proposal or an Invitation to Tender. In either case a closing date needs to be decided and notified. A Request for Proposal is the most cost effective method.

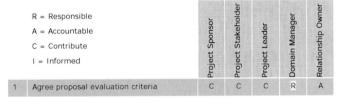

> *An Invitation to Tender is used only in situations where there are multiple suppliers competing for the same major piece of work.*
>
> *A tendering process needs to be managed by people with specialist procurement skills to ensure success.*

With a Request for Proposal approach, the selected supplier needs to understand that the situation will not become competitive with other suppliers, providing they submit a quotation that is acceptable in respect of quality, price, delivery and service.

It is useful to nominate a reserve supplier to help your bargaining position and in case negotiations collapse. Do not invite the reserve supplier to propose unless a collapse situation occurs. It is demotivating and a waste of money for the supplier if they do not win the business and can jeopardise the relationship with your organisation.

3	Evaluate responses and select supplier		I	I	C	R	A

There are two aspects to proposal evaluation - objective and subjective – both of which are often needed. The results need to be documented for evidence.

Objective evaluation involves your assessment of the supplier's capability to deliver to the Terms of Reference and meet the requirement as specified. For each function or requirement, can the supplier meet it in total, in part or not at all. Price, delivery and service are assessed objectively.

Subjective evaluation is about 'buying the people', for example:

- Has the organisation or anyone you know worked with the people before?
- Are they innovative?
- Will they be easy to do business with?
- Do you like their attitude?
- Do you trust them?

To perform subjective evaluation:

- Identify the options
- State, for each option, the advantages, disadvantages, cost considerations and risks
- Select a preferred and reserve option
- Prepare a case for the preferred option
- Agree the case with the sponsor, stakeholders and customer.

Proposal Evaluation Checklist

1	Are the evaluation criteria decided?
2	Do the evaluation criteria need to be agreed with the Project Sponsor and Project Stakeholders?
3	Is a Request for Proposal adequate or is an Invitation to Tender needed?
4	If an Invitation to Tender is needed, has expert advice and guidance been solicited?
5	Has a Request for Proposal or Invitation to Tender been communicated the selected supplier?
6	Has a timely response been received?
7	Has the proposal or tender response been evaluated and does it meet the evaluation criteria?
8	Does the supplier's proposal state any assumptions they are making?
9	How much of their turnover does your business represent to the supplier? If greater than 30%, is this a risk?
10	Has a supplier been selected for contract negotiation and a reserve supplier nominated?

Contract Agreement

An agreement might range from a simple 'Letter of Agreement' to a fully-fledged legal contract. Typically it would include:

- A list of the deliverables to be created by the supplier and the delivery deadlines to be met
- Reference to the development method and quality standards which the deliverables need to satisfy
- Prices
- A schedule of payments that is fair and enforceable based on agreed performance measures
- Reference to the processes for issues, risks and changes
- A statement of the escalation paths and levels
- A statement of the processes for monitoring and reporting performance.
- The agreed supplier Terms of Business

So that a supplier can provide services before full funding is approved, a letter of agreement can be signed, providing the cost is covered by initial funding.

Steps

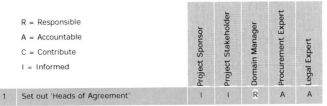

R = Responsible
A = Accountable
C = Contribute
I = Informed

		Project Sponsor	Project Stakeholder	Domain Manager	Procurement Expert	Legal Expert
1	Set out 'Heads of Agreement'	I	I	R	A	A

Agreements with external suppliers must conform to the policy and processes of your organisation. Before starting, ask for the help and guidance from your legal and procurement functions.

Decide the topics that need to be convered by the contract and state what you want to achieve.

Be aware of the project's stages and the possible points at which the supplier contract might need to be terminated prematurely or any circumstances at which you might need to de-commit from the contract.

Discuss the Heads of Agreement with the supplier and resolve any misunderstandings.

2	Agree contract details			R	A	A

To be legally sustainable, a contract must be precise, unambiguous and fair to both sides. Obtain a suitable and relevant, standard form of contract from the organisation's Knowledge Library and, with the help of the procurement and legal functions, tailor this to embrace the Heads of Agreement.

3	Negotiate contract terms, costs & services				R	A	A

A skilled negotiator needs to negotiate the contract with the supplier. If price, quality and delivery are of paramount importance, a 'Cooperative Contract' is fierce but it might be a good option. See Techniques.

4	Agree escalation trees				R	A	A

Agree a co-ordinated line of escalation within the supplier and customer organisation.

5	Identify the critical success factors and prime measures				R	A	A

Identify the areas of contract sensitivity and decide if they are critical to the success of the agreement. With critical success factors, the fewer the better - up to six is OK but certainly no more than twelve. Decide the prime measure of each critical success factor and the normal state or limits within which it must be maintained. These targets are the supplier performance measures.

By now, the contract should be ready for signing.

> *A contract can only be signed after the Change Board has sanctioned full funding. The aim should be to have it ready for signature by the end of High Level Planning.*

6	Update Supplier Portfolio				C	R	

If a new external supplier relationship is to continue after the project is closed, this work of managing this should be delegated to the manager of an appropriate business-as-usual function.

Contract Negotiation

> *If a contract isn't profitable it's unreasonable to expect a supplier to be enthusiastic about delivery.*

Negotiation is a two-way process of give and take. In its simplest form it is based around six secret 'prices', three for the customer and three for the supplier.

The customer knows the absolute top price they would be prepared to pay and the bargain price they would love to get it for. The supplier knows the absolute bottom price they would accept and the price they would love to get for it. If these price ranges do not overlap one or other party will eventually walk away.

If the price ranges do overlap a fruitful negotiation usually happens that will end in a third price being agreed, which is the same for both customer and supplier – the negotiated price. This process creates a sense of value and satisfaction for both parties.

Here are some easy guidelines you can follow:

- Decide the negotiation team - elect one, skilled person to lead the negotiation and act as spokesperson, team member views should be expressed only in consultation sessions

- Refuse to be hassled into reaching agreement – adopt a 'stone face, black heart' negotiation style

- Conduct a negotiation as a series of sprints, not as a marathon – call regular 'time-outs' for consultation

- When conceding, never make two concessions in succession - always ask for a concession in return for a concession

- Look for concessions in areas other than price that are of value to the organisation

- Seek to arrive at a 'win-win' deal where both parties feel they obtained the best possible price.

Contract Agreement Checklist

1	Does the agreement conform to your organisation's policies and processes?
2	Are the Heads of Agreement fit for purpose?
3	Will the customer and supplier benefit, fairly?
4	Will the contract enable you to control the things that are critical for project success - quality, specification, price and delivery?
5	Are the de-commit points in the project the same as those in the supplier's agreement, so that should this arise it will not be disputed?
6	Have the escalation paths been agreed?
7	Have performance measures been agreed, are the mechanisms for monitoring performance in place?
8	Has the Change Board sanctioned full funding and is the supplier's agreement signed?
9	Has the Supplier Portfolio been updated?

Tips

- Appoint a person in the organisation who is empowered to negotiate commercial arrangements, resolve contractual terms and manage relationship issues

- Get each supplier to nominate an empowered person to negotiate commercial arrangements, resolve contractual terms, manage relationship issues, schedule resources and negotiate delivery promises

- Before engaging an external supplier, check to ensure there is no conflict of interest with the third party supplier products they will be working with - failure to do this may risk a breach of contract for which the organisation is liable

- Involve in the negotiation the customer domain manager who will inherit the deliverables or the consequences of the services provided

- Don't assume internal and external suppliers understand your approach and what you must achieve

- Don't decide to invest on price alone

- Don't make sourcing decisions on a piecemeal basis without checking fit to the overall design or architecture

- Don't ignore the advice of subject matter experts who understand the supply-side risks

- Let the supplier decide their project management methodology and how they deliver their own activities but insist that they conform to your minimum planning and reporting requirements, and formats

- Agree and communicate a policy for reward and recognition common to all internal and external suppliers, and the organisation as a whole

- Have clear policy guidelines for engaging, managing and disengaging consultants and contractors

- Services from internal suppliers may be cross-charged to your project in a devolved responsibility organisation – is this properly represented in the Cost Benefit Analysis?

Communication Management

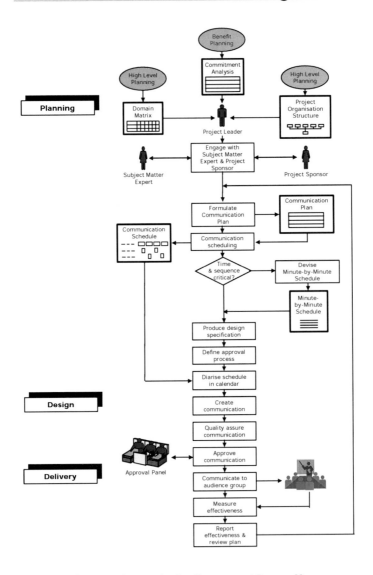

Figure 27: Communication Management Process Map

Communication Management is the process by which a Communication Plan is planned, designed and delivered.

> *A **Communication Plan** is a schedule of timely communications that uses a variety of channels and media to ensure people understand the reasons for change, how it will be implemented, and how it will impact them personally or the groups they represent.*

A Communication Plan should be considered as a deliverable of every project.

The Project Sponsor is responsible for communications to impacted audience groups, although the Project Leader will almost certainly formulate the plan and co-ordinate delivery.

The scale of the Communication Plan needed depends on the organisational impact, external impact and surrounding sensitivities of the project. The primary focus is the audience groups included in Stakeholder Analysis and the Commitment Analysis.

Figure 28 illustrates a suggested schema for the creation and delivery of a complex Communication Plan. This should be adapted to suit the impact of the project.

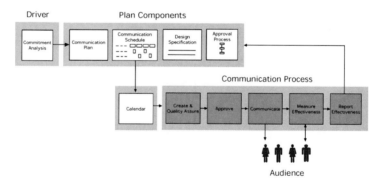

Figure 28: Communication Plan Schema

In all cases, the Project Leader should engage with a subject matter expert or internal supplier domain with the capability, skills and resources to create, and deliver quality communications.

The following sets out what the Project Leader needs to consider when working with a subject matter expert to plan, design and deliver a Communication Plan.

Planning

Plan Formulation

The Communication Plan needs to be formulated considering all of the following in relation to the scope of the project:

- **Information Types** - each organisation will have a set of information types which it needs to communicate, for example:

• Strategy	• Management information
• Benefits	• Status and progress
• Plans	• Processes
• Organisation structure	• Performance statistics
• Topic or subject briefing	

- **Audience Groups** - the different audience groups to which information is communicated, including:

• Corporate management	• Suppliers
• Corporate staff	• Intermediaries
• Executive management	• Associates
• Leadership team	• General public
• Staff	• Media (press, TV, etc.)
• Unions & staff associations	• Competitors
• Customers	

- **Communication Channels** - range channels through which communication can be directed, including:

Public	Group	Individual
• TV broadcast	• Presentation	• Surface mail
• Radio broadcast	• E-mail	• E-mail
• Internet	• Newsletter	• Questionnaire
• Exhibitions	• Intranet	• One-to-one
• Editorial	• Event	
• Advertising	• Roadshow	
	• Seminar	
	• Street-stand	

- **Communication Medium** – appropriate to the information type and the communication channel chosen, including:

• Narrative
• Prepared script
• Brochureware
• DVD

© Verdandi Limited 1984-2010

Steps

		Project Sponsor	Domain Manager	Project Leader	Project Partner	Head of Chnage
R = Responsible A = Accountable C = Contribute I = Informed						
1	Formulate Communication Plan	R	C	A	A	I

Working with a subject matter expert and the Project Sponsor, the Project Leader needs to make sure that all communications from the project to relevant audience groups are included in the Communication Plan. Audience groups relevant to the project are identified in the Domain Matrix and the Project Organisation Structure.

The manpower and money needed to prepare and deliver the entire Communication Plan must be estimated to ensure the plan is affordable.

2	Communication scheduling	R	C	A	A	I

The communication schedule is an appendix to the Communication Plan. It shows the frequency and timing of communication to the different audience groups in a graphical format over time.

Timing and sequence of communication may be critical. Where this is the case a Minute-by-Minute Schedule should be devised by the Project Leader to control the sequence and timing of communication delivery and to rehearse this with the communication delivery team.

3	Produce design specification	R	C	A	A	I

This appendix to the Communication Plan specifies any design criteria that need to be adhered to when creating communications in different mediums.

4	Approval process definition	R	C	A	A	I

Define an approval process appropriate to the sensitivity of the communications and include as an appendix to the Communication Plan.

5	Diarise schedule in calendar	R	C	A	A	I

The communication schedule should be diarised and triggered by an alarm, so that the person responsible for planning and preparing each communication is alerted in advance and can start the preparation in good time to meet the delivery deadline.

It is important for the person responsible for delivering a communication to diarise the event and for the person responsible for the schedule to confirm that the event has occurred. Co-ordinating delivery of the communication schedule may be made the responsibility of the Change Office.

Planning Checklist

1	Does the Communication Plan address the areas of perceived resistance in the Commitment Analysis?
2	Have the domains responsible for communication within the organisation been engaged with regard to creation of the Communication Plan?
3	Has the necessary approval process been considered?
4	Has the communication schedule been diarised?
5	Is the Communication Plan affordable?

Design

To fulfil its purpose, each communication needs to create advocacy and support. To achieve this it needs to be principled, conveying necessary messages in a way that recognises the need to manage people's uncertainty during periods of change.

The content of each communication needs to be planned, scripted and professionally produced in relation to the information type involved, the audience group being targeted, and appropriate to the channel and medium being used.

- Communications need to be created taking into account feedback from earlier communications
- Any communication impacting people requires full consultation with the organisation's HR function, prior to publication
- Whenever information is distributed external to the organisation, advice must be sought from the organisation's communications and public relations functions prior to preparation and delivery
- Each communication must be co-ordinated, so that messages are consistent, with all elements of the communications mix considered within each communication.

Steps

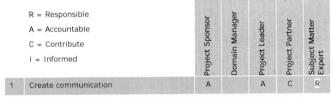

	R = Responsible A = Accountable C = Contribute I = Informed	Project Sponsor	Domain Manager	Project Leader	Project Partner	Subject Matter Expert
1	Create communication	A		A	C	R

When creating an individual communication, the key questions to consider are:

- What is the aim of the communication?
- What are the audience groups to which the messages are targeted?
- What are the messages to be communicated?
- What is the purpose and value of each message?
- Who are the specific members within these groups to whom the messages are targeted?
- Will the audience groups want to know or will they be interested in this information?
- Is it pertinent that the audience group shares this information, for example, timing of changes?
- What channels are to be used?
- What medium will be used?
- When does it need to be communicated?
- Is it necessary to follow-up communications to judge effectiveness?
- Is feedback expected?

© Verdandi Limited 1984-2010

2	Quality assure communication		R		C	C	A

Each communication must be quality assured to ensure it is fit for intended purpose and free of defects. This is a suggested checklist:

- Aligned - to the organisation's brand and corporate image

- Supportive - of the organisation's goal and strategic imperatives

- Effectively targeted - at audiences and people to whom it is relevant

- Efficient – avoid wasting natural resources

- Honest - when information cannot be given, this should be explained

- Timely - shared as soon as possible with those whom it effects, to help to minimise rumours

- Clear and concise – avoiding jargon and easily understood by the target audience

- Structured – categorised to make the general content, theme and importance easily identifiable

- Engaging – written and presented in a way that is informative, influencing, consultative and appealing to the recipient

- Motivating - engendering a sense of unity, identity, and pride in the organisation

- People sensitive - showing empathy and with due consideration given to employee relations;

- Equal opportunities sensitive – meeting people's needs given regional, cultural or other differences

- Inclusive – advising external and associated audiences within appropriate timeframes

- Credible - delivered professionally, by credible people, through appropriate channels, using an effective medium

- Secure – not revealing confidential information to people who might use it to the disadvantage of the organisation

- Compliant – with legal, regulatory or statutory requirements

- Setting expectations - for further communication and information where appropriate

- Usable - when feedback is required, presenting in a way that makes response easy.

3	Approve communication		R	C	A	A	I

If the change to which the Communication Plan relates is of a critical or sensitive nature, a panel, comprising the Project Sponsor and selected Project Stakeholders may need to approve all communications.

Delivery

The Project Leader needs to make sure that communications are prepared in good time and delivered in accordance with the schedule, with their effectiveness measured and feedback actioned.

If necessary, the Communication Plan and project deliverables should be altered until advocacy and support for benefit realisation is achieved.

Steps

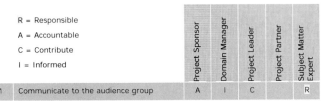

		Project Sponsor	Domain Manager	Project Leader	Project Partner	Subject Matter Expert
1	Communicate to the audience group	A	I	C		R

If the communication medium is personal, skilled communicators need to deliver the content; people who have received appropriate training, coaching and mentoring.

If the communication medium is impersonal, for example a DVD, communications professionals should produce the DVD.

2	Measure effectiveness	A	C	C		R

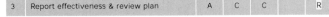

Where a communication may be sensitive to internal and external opinion, ensure the necessary feedback channels and processes been created and tested, and how to access them has been included in the communication.

If needed, describe how the communication will be followed-up to judge:

- If it was received and understood

- How was it received

- The anticipated impact of the message versus actual impact.

3	Report effectiveness & review plan	A	C	C		R

Channel feedback into the communication planning and design processes.

Delivery Checklist

1	Has the domain responsible for communication within the organisation been engaged with regard to creation of the Communication Plan?
2	Does the Communication Plan address the areas of perceived resistance in the Commitment Analysis?
3	Has effectiveness been measured, reported and action taken?

Tips

- Achieve commitment through communication
- Poor or inappropriate communication is probably worse than none
- Time communication for maximum effect otherwise its value diminishes

Techniques

The following techniques are commonly applied throughout
Successful Project Management.

Interviewing

An interview, in the context of Successful Project Management,
aims to:

- Understand the interviewee's role within the organisation
- Elicit the interviewee's own vision, views and expectations
- Assist the interviewee in better comprehending the project
  context.

Interview questions should be sent to the interviewee before the
interview. Any information about the interviewee acquired in
advance will add value to the conduct of the interview.

It is usually more effective for the interviewer to conduct an
interview with a partner. One concentrates on questioning and
interpersonal communication, the other on accurately recording
responses and detecting the interviewee's sensory reactions. If
there is inconsistency, the second person can pick this up and
suggest paraphrasing to get the clarity needed. Drawing upon the
skills and knowledge of two people will both improve the quality of
the interview and speed up the process.

Before starting the interview, check that your interpersonal
communication skills are 'switched on' so you can gauge how the
interviewee is thinking and reacting.

Ask questions in the order planned. You can allow the interviewee
to deviate but make sure that all planned questions are asked. Be
ready and able to explain the meaning of any terminology you use
such as, vision, strategic imperative or objective.

Questions should be 'open' and delivered in a conversational
manner:

- 'Why?' is used to challenge someone's values or beliefs
- 'What?' and 'How?' are used to solicit ideas and opinions
- 'Who?' 'When?' and 'Where?' are used to gather facts

If questions are not relevant, record that the interviewee has no
view. If answers are not forthcoming to relevant questions, offer to
return to the question. If the answers are insufficient, use the verbs
'tell me', 'explain' and 'describe' to drill-down further.

It is reasonable to challenge the view of the interviewee providing
this intervention is seen as helpful and not directive or dismissive -
It is the interviewer's job to draw-out answers, not to convince.

Closed questions, requiring a 'yes or no' answer, are used to switch
subject. Leading, multiple and hypothetical questions should be
avoided.

Version Control

Version control is a method of numbering editions of deliverables to avoid confusion when building iterations or when making corrections and changes. It should be considered a necessary discipline, not bureaucracy.

Version Number

The version number is made up of a release and revision - together referred to as the version number. The recommended format of version number is N.N. The first digit represents the release that, when increased, shows a major change has taken place to the deliverable. The second digit represents the revision that, when increased, shows that a minor change has taken place.

Build Number

When a deliverable is constructed through a series of iterations, a third number is added to indicate the build iteration. For example, where a deliverable is being created for the first time, the version will be release 0, revision 0, build 1, i.e. 0.0.1, the second iteration will be version 0.0.2 and so on. When the final iteration has been approved the deliverable is frozen, the release or revision increased by 1, and the build number dropped (e.g. version 0.0.14 becomes version 1.0). Any changes to the deliverable from this point on must be managed using the Change Control process.

New Versions

When it is agreed to modify an existing document or deliverable, it becomes necessary to change the version. If it is judged to be a minor change then the revision is updated. If it is judged to be a major change then the release is updated.

As soon as an existing deliverable is changed the build number is once again added to the end of the version number. For example, if version 1.0 is changed then the next build iteration becomes 1.0.1. When the build process is complete for a minor change the version number becomes version 1.1, and for a major change the version number becomes 2.0.

The person making a change always to update the version number as part of the change process. Any tangible deliverable that does not conform to this policy should be rejected by recipients and drawn to the creator's attention.

Workshop Facilitation Guidelines

A workshop is a facilitated gathering of relevant experts with a declared aim or objectives, used to collect ideas and information or arrive at recommendations.

The declared aim or objectives of the workshop and agenda should always be agreed before it starts. During the project, expect to organise:

- **Definition Workshop** - attended by the Project Sponsor and Project Stakeholders, it aims to resolve inconsistencies and ambiguities, and unanimously agree the objectives and scope
- **Benefit Workshop** - attended by the Business Owner, Project Stakeholders and customer domain managers, it aims to:
  - Determine the dependencies between strategic imperatives, benefits, objectives and proposed changes
  - Quantify the benefits
  - Agree the ownership and realisation timetable and ownership of each benefit.
- **Deliverable Workshop** - attended by people representing the project suppliers and customers that identifies the deliverables to be created by the project to a level of detail adequate for further planning
- **Risk Workshop** - attended by relevant experts, it aims to advance the application of the risk management process
- **Quality Assurance Workshop** - attended by relevant individuals, it aims to review a deliverable against its specification and quality standards, and unanimously agree its deficiencies in time for them to be corrected.

Any information to be worked upon should be distributed in advance so that participants can form their own views.

At the workshop, agree the behavioural guidelines with the participants. Behaviours that make for a good workshop include:

- Start and end on time
- All working to a common aim or objectives
- Everyone must have the opportunity to participate
- Open communication
- One person speaking at a time
- Start transactions with a question
- Precise wording and consistent use
- Jargon and abbreviations must be explained
- Any information to be worked on must be distributed in advance so that participants can form their own opinions
- If you don't know the answer, don't guess, just say "I can find out" – this is an acceptable response

- Adult-to-adult communication.

The facilitator ensures the smooth flow through the agenda, intervening only if:

- Discussion becomes destructively heated
- Anyone becomes emotionally upset
- There is verbal aggression or bullying.

The co-facilitator ensures conformance to the agenda and records outcomes using interactive media to display information, for example, PC and projector, flipchart or 'Post-It' pads.

Any issues that cannot be quickly and easily managed within the workshop should be recorded buy the co-facilitator in a 'Car Park' of actions to be taken outside the workshop.

Each issue within the Car Park should be reviewed at the end of the workshop to see if it can be resolved, if not, it should be the responsibility of one named person to escalate together with a target date when a resolution should be achieved. When difficult decisions need to be taken, the person ultimately responsible needs to make the final decision if a consensus cannot be reached.

Workshops should last no more than two hours. If agreement cannot be reached easily, take a one-hour break and reconvene.

Working with a Development Method

A development method is a documented, systematic and proven way of completing work, used to guide the efficient creation of a complex deliverable. They commence at the very outset of the work and are applied using Successful Project Management.

What all development methods have in common, from the very simplest like a cookbook recipe to the most complex is that they follow similar, 'broad-brush' stages. These guide you not to:

- Design and specify something until you have the conceptual requirements

- Build and test it until you have designed and specified it

- Operationally prove it until it has been built and tested

- Pilot it until it until it has been operationally proven

- Roll it out until it has been piloted.

To demystify the concept of working with a development method and show the wisdom contained within; the following example explains how a development method for building a complex new product around a new IT application might be applied:

Conceptual Requirements

This is where the conceptual design of a key deliverable is specified and communicated by subject matter experts so that feasibility can be researched and viability confirmed.

A conceptual design might include illustrated designs, storyboards, drawings, models, narrative, costings - in fact anything that can be quickly and cost-effectively produced that will help bring the concept to life for evaluation by prospective users or customers. The product is a Design Specification.

Inevitably, proving the conceptual design will involve market research.

> ***Market research is the process of determining need or stimulating awareness so as to establish that there is customer demand, and a sustainable business case.***

Design & Specification

This involves production the detailed functional and technical specifications of the key deliverable in support of the Design Specification. It includes:

- Functional Specification – a list of the features and designed actions that are necessary for a key deliverable to be fit for purpose

- Technical Specification – a description of the specific technical environment in which the deliverable must operate.

The design, functional and technical specifications together make up the Requirements Specification, which is used to control the building and testing of the key deliverable.

Specification involves:

- Establishing needs - by interview, survey, analysis or measurement

- Insisting on having things explained so they can be easily understood

- Taking independent advice if not confident of the explanation given

- Agreeing the requirements with the customer

- Ranking each requirement in terms of importance.

Creation and agreement of the Requirements Specification usually requires the services of a Business Analyst.

Build & Test

Solution Selection

Solution selection involves deciding which ready-made solution will best meet a given specification from a number of different options. This is based on objective evaluation. If there is more than one proposal that fully meets the specification, subjective evaluation is used to differentiate them.

These techniques are explained in the 'Proposal Evaluation' section of Supplier Engagement.

Prototyping

Prototyping techniques can be applied to confirm functionality when there is uncertainty regarding the suitability of a specified solution, for instance if it represents something that is new or unknown to the organisation.

Prototyping creates successive pictures, physical models and working versions of a deliverable to show design functionality in a low cost, visible form to reveal any modifications which may be necessary prior to incurring the full cost of building, testing and proving the solution. For example:

- Drawing an 'artist's impression', preparing a 'straw-man' or 'storyboard' to show the customer

- Building a model to show the customer

- Assembling a working prototype and demonstrating it to the customer in a model environment.

Prototyping aims to minimise the paper design and maximise the modelling. A prototype is preferable to a series of low-visual-impact technical specifications that are difficult for a customer to understand.

Prototypes are best experienced in a 'model environment'. A model environment is a temporary physical environment created to enable the customer to experience a working prototype of a deliverable in context so they can judge functional suitability. Early production of operational processes and delivery of this to the model environment will ensure that the solution being delivered meets operational needs.

A model environment may be needed if:

- There is a range of complex and integrated deliverables

- A deliverable will have a large impact on the processes of an organisation.

If needed, a model environment is made a deliverable.

Use of prototyping needs to be contained so as to gain maximum value yet meet the progress expectations of the Project Sponsor.

Operational Proving

Testing

Testing starts at the Build & Test stage and continues through Operational Proving. Testing is a process of checking functionality, usability and acceptability against specification and quality standards by a number of people with different vested interests in the outcome, for example:

- Suppliers

- Project Team

- Customers or Users

All these groups are involved throughout.

Testing is about reducing the risk associated with introducing a change not about testing to perfection and finding all the errors.

In complex environments, testing may require an equivalent amount of manpower and time to that of the creation process. A test strategy and a test plan are required deliverables.

A test strategy is a holistic view that sets out when testing will start and how it will be performed, given the operational imperatives, and the realities of the environment in which testing will take place.

A test plan is a precise schedule of why, when, where and how testing will take place, and using whom and what processes and tools.

The test plan can be developed as the project advances, providing it is available in time for testing.

The need for testing rises exponentially in relation to the number of people using a solution and the attitude of the customer towards the solution. Experience has shown:

- If a deliverable of given complexity is created for personal use it can take the same amount of time to test it thoroughly as it takes to create it, so that it is fit for the author to use

- If the same deliverable is created for use by a group of people, they will not be as tolerant as the author and consequently testing can take a number of times longer than creation, for example, it may it may take ten times as long in the case of a complex deliverable

- If the same deliverable is created for use by the general public, where public liability is at stake, testing can take many times longer than creation, for example, it may take one hundred times as long to test the software for a fly-by-wire aircraft.

When planning for testing there are a number of activities that can be scheduled that will cause suppliers to be attentive to detail during creation.

If this thorough approach to test planning does not avoid problems, by making people think twice before they act, it will cause sufficient time and manpower to be set aside to address these situations.

The key point is to plan to be radical in the approach to testing as well as thorough in the level of testing applied. It should be remembered that the customer is always the final quality assurance checkpoint.

Unit Testing

Whatever the supplier claims about the deliverable in the agreed specification, test plans should be constructed to test the claim. For example, if it claimed that that the deliverable can be dropped from one meter onto a concrete surface without breaking then plan to test that feature.

Linked Trials

Plan to test individual deliverables and then plan to test them in combination. For example, if literature is being created plan to check that the literature will fit into the folders designed to hold them and that they have not been made the same size. When complex systems are involved, the possibility that things will work in isolation but not in combination is almost guaranteed.

Volume Testing

Plan to conduct tests on the linked environment with simulated volumes of transactions. This will draw out performance, capacity and throughput problems that would otherwise not emerge.

Resilience Testing

Where equipment is involved, plan to unplug each component and switch off each power source in turn to see the effect on operation. If resilience was specified in the solution this will be tested.

Make sure that if automatic fallback systems are specified and installed that they are tested not only for working in the event of a fallback situation but that they operate in fallback mode for the specified duration and, when exhausted, can be quickly restored to their automatic fallback status.

Regression Testing

If, following the final testing, there is doubt regarding the stability or performance of the solution, a full regression test may be needed. This may mean repeating the entire testing process after actions have been taken to rectify the stability and performance problems.

Backup & Recovery

All solutions involving computer-based technology will require backup and recovery systems. These need to be set up along with the supporting processes and procedures. A full-scale disaster recovery rehearsal should be staged before the solution is put into operation.

Support & Maintenance

All solutions where support and maintenance has been specified require tests to be performed on the quality of service response prior to handover to the customer.

Implementation

Implementation Planning

Business-as-usual will need to prepare itself for implementation and handover. This may be a separate and significant project in its own right for the customer that needs to start well before implementation commences.

Activities should be included in the Task & Activity List that places responsibility on a Project Team Member to pre-check that everything needed for implementation exists, and is fit for intended purpose. This will mitigate the risk of failure considerably.

If a new process is being created or an existing process changed, there should be a clearly agreed handover point where the project team activities cease and operational activities start.

Once a solution is live, operational change control will take over and performance monitored against critical success factor prime measures. These are established as part of the project.

Release Management

Release Management is a process used to minimise the disruption of implementing a range of improvements to a complex operating environment by marshalling together number of deliverables from separate projects and implementing them at one time, on the most appropriate and least disruptive date.

Release cutover dates may be time or event driven. A schedule of release cutover dates should be communicated in advance so that:

- Project Leaders can plan to meet the delivery deadline and ensure the collective integrity of the deliverables

- Customers can prepare and organise themselves for the acceptance, handover and changed operation

- Suppliers can organise resources to support the cutover and the agreed period of warranty.

Cutover

It is wise for the cutover to be rehearsed, perhaps several times, so that risk of failure is minimised. A back-out plan is also needed for use in the event of failure. It is best to accommodate all the above in a release management project.

Pilot Implementation

A pilot is a full-scale test of the release version of a solution in a representative situation with real volumes. It is used to prove a finished solution that will be implemented more widely. The finished solution will sometimes need to be piloted in one or more representative situations in order to prove its acceptability to the satisfaction of the customer

Piloting is always recommended when multiple implementations of a finished solution need to planned and executed.

The purpose of piloting is to prove that the:

- Release version of the solution operates as expected and that it works in a quality manner

- Systems for controlling change and distributing changes work effectively

- Maintenance and support functions and processes work effectively

- Plans for roll-out of the finished solution are defect free and fit for intended purpose.

Full Implementation

The release version of the solution should be rolled-out only after the pilot(s) have been proven. Quality is put at risk if solutions are rolled-out before pilots are proven. The cost consequences of this can be very significant in terms of customer satisfaction and discontent. Managing the transition from the old system to a new system can be implemented in a number of ways.

The method by which transition is achieved is the Project Sponsor's choice. The situation, however, usually dictates the choice of approach:

- Burn the Bridges - no cutover or fallback options are catered for. This is the easiest to operate and has the lowest cost but the highest risk of failure.

- Cutover with Fallback - there is an option to recover to the original state should a failure occur during implementation. This is medium cost to operate with medium risk of failure.

- Migration - where a large entity is to be changed, it is segmented into stages and migrated stage at a time to minimise impact of failure, for example migrating a database, A's first, B-E's second, F-L's third, etcetera. If at any stage migration fails, revert back to the previous successful state.

- Parallel Run - the new and the old are run in parallel and results compared for accuracy before committing to the new environment. This option is the most costly to operate but has the least risk of failure.

Cooperative Contract

A Cooperative Contract is a form of supplier agreement that has incentives to inspire the supplier to willingly deliver on time and improve quality throughout the contract term.

The following questions are presented to the supplier who must give affirmative or quantified answers to all questions or walk away, whereupon another supplier is selected.

1   Will you work with us to agree a specification that will form a binding part of the agreement?

2   Given your present capabilities, including the people you employ and the processes and systems you use, what is the maximum number of defects that we can expect within a measured volume of work you deliver to us?

3   Progressing to zero defects is our aim - at this stage, if the maximum number of defects is acceptable to us is it reasonable for you?

4   What percentage margin do you think is reasonable for your industry and are you prepared to work to this for the duration of the contract?

5   Are you prepared to reveal your actual percentage margin to us?

6   If we give you a rolling, forward delivery schedule, are you prepared to promise to deliver 'just-in-time'?

7   Can we agree hard, firm and soft zone 'time-fences' within the rolling, forward delivery schedule, and the respective owners of each zone?

- The hard zone will remain fixed unless the supplier zone owner willingly agrees to the change

- The firm zone will only change with the permission of the customer zone owner

- The soft zone can be changed without referral

8   Can we freely and actively exchange ideas for improvement of each other's processes and systems?

9   Do you understand what we mean by a delivery promise - quality work, on time and using the agreed resource, and are you prepared to abide by this?

10   If you exceed the agreed defect limit or deliver late three times, then we will terminate the contract – do you agree that this is fair?

The supplier is expected to use some of the percentage margin to invest in continual improvement and so improve quality and reduce cost. Consequently, any advantage gained by the supplier is shared automatically with the customer.

Using a Steering Committee

A Steering Committee is a panel of selected stakeholders chaired by the Programme Sponsor with the Programme Director and Programme Manager as members, formed to validate, advocate, monitor and guide a programme in relation to strategic imperatives and realisation of benefits.

For a large-scale project the members are the Project Sponsor, selected Project Stakeholders and the leader, and the partner of the master project.

Steering Committee Responsibilities

1 Agreeing:

- The Programme Vision
- Programme objectives and scope
- Business Case and subsequent revisions
- Manpower and skills to be deployed
- Necessary investment in project management
- The major development methods and quality standards to be followed
- Supplier proposals
- The need for and frequency of reviews and audits
- That key deliverables are of an acceptable standard.

2 Deciding:

- Programme structure
- Priorities
- Options
- To re-scope or terminate the programme, if appropriate.

3 Governance of projects within the programme

4 Sanctioning major expenditure and contingency allowances

5 Assisting with the resolution of persistent issues

6 Guiding on action to be taken on high and unacceptable risks

7 Authorising changes to the programme objectives, scope, schedule, costs, benefits or timescales

8   Reviewing:

- The progress and status of the programme and projects making up the programme, to ensure it remains viable and on course in relation to strategic imperatives, objectives, critical success factors, costs and benefits

- Sensitive communications and any other documents that impact the overall programme

- The need for and timing of major changes to the organisation

- Status in relation to de-commit criteria

Steering Committee Agenda

The agenda for a Steering Committee meeting typically includes:

1   Checkpoint Reviews - evolving as the programme progresses through its six-stage lifecycle:

- Programme inception - agreeing the organisation and structure

- Strategy Communication - understanding the challenge and opportunity

- Pathfinding – agreeing the analysis and findings, and deciding options

- Mobilising - agreeing the resources

- Programme Delivery - Stage Review of programme viability

- Programme Closure - Agreeing plans for benefit realisation and the management of risks Governance.

2   Governance – review gates apply to the programme's master project and to each project making up the programme:

- Gate 1 - Bid Assessment

- Gate 2 - Feasibility & Viability

- Gate 3 - Full funding

- Gate 4 - Closure Approval

3   External impacts and interdependencies

4   Programme progress and status

5   Review of individual project progress and status, by exception

6   Communication review.

Organisation Design

For a change environment to be effective, the organisation design needs to take into account the scale of change taking place and the maturity of the organisation.

For example, an established organisation that is transforming to a new operating model over a sustained period might need an organisation design similar to that illustrated in Figure 29.

In a large group, where responsibility for prioritising the budget for discretionary spend is devolved to business units, each business unit would need to establish its own organisation design, tailored to its local needs, and balanced with centrally provided services.

In a smaller organisation, all the roles and responsibilities are still relevant but need to be performed by fewer people, perhaps holding multiple roles.

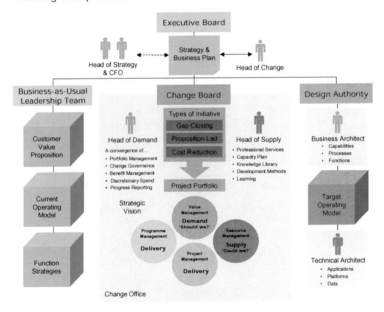

Figure 29: Organisation Design

The Value and Resource Management processes are operated by the Change Office, and used to conduct the flow of ideas and underpin the demand (Should we?) and supply (Could we?) equation.

Roles within the change environment structure are described in the section 'Roles'. Key role holders including Head of Change, Head of Demand and Head of Supply will typically be members of the Change Board.

Service Delivery

People delivering projects and programmes and providing professional services will be organised in different ways, dependent upon the needs of the organisation.

Delivery Practice Model

This is where an elite group of professional services practitioners are employed within a fully funded function.

Typical characteristics are:

- Resident practitioners uphold the standards and carry out professional development duties as partners, coaches and mentors, as well as taking on their own delivery roles.

- People may be seconded into the practice for a 'tour of duty' as full-time programme or project managers before taking up a new business-as-usual leadership role.

- Business Analysts, who have a detailed understanding of the organisation's processes and systems, might be assigned to Executive Sponsors to help them formulate their segment of the project portfolio and guide Business Owners in taking ideas through the Value Management.

- Services are re-charged to the functions of the organisation on a commercial basis.

This model is often preferred in organisations where there is a sustained demand for high-capability professional services resources over an indefinite period.

Community of Practice Model

> **A Community of Practice is a cross-functional common interest group, comprising professional and occasional practitioners who have a job need to collaborate, and share knowledge, expertise and experience for mutual benefit.**

This model is suited to an environment where discretionary spend is variable and leadership capability is seen as a necessary management discipline.

The structure has three layers:

- Core - People who, as a rule of thumb, spend greater than 70% of their time working on projects. It includes people who support the community, administer the project community website and govern the environment

- Involved – People who spend between 20% and 70% of their time working on projects

- Interested – People who spend less than 20% of their time working on projects.

With this model, people are employed within and paid for by the functions of the organisation, supported by a small, fully funded, central coordination team. In this environment, people can easily move between business-as-usual leadership and change leadership roles through time, as their careers develop.

The key to the success is the level of passion and engagement of the participants, plus a desire to contribute, improve and share.

Project Community Website

> *A Project Community Website, maintained by the Change Office, provides a one-stop, self-service shop for the organisation's programme and project related information.*

Information in a Project Community Website includes:

- Current programmes and projects

- Progress and status reports

- Tools

- Best practice processes

- Development methods

- Reusable knowledge.

It includes space where people can:

- Advertise their own capabilities, knowledge and skills

- Discuss project and programme related issues

- Collaborate with others

- Access related self-development courses and materials.

A hybrid structure is where a core team, organised as a Delivery Practice, provides the sustainability to cope with continual demand and a Community of Practice the flexibility to absorb exceptional demand.

Roles

The following table lists all the roles and responsibilities within change management.

Role	Definition
Benefit Facilitator	A person conversant with the Target Operating Model and systems of the organisation, such as a Business Analyst, empowered by the Head of Change who supports an Executive Sponsor, and Business Owners by: • Managing a section of the project portfolio on behalf of the Executive Sponsor • Hosting the processing of new ideas • Supporting the preparation of Bids • Facilitating Benefit Workshops • Expediting realisation of benefits.
Benefit Owner	A customer domain manager who accepts responsibility for realising a project benefit, and who: • Makes a personal commitment to benefit realisation • Plans the realisation of the benefit • Negotiates the benefit amount and realisation date • Acts to realise the benefit.
Business Architect	A senior Business Analyst responsible for ensuring the conceptual integrity of the Target Operating Model in relation to the strategy, Customer Value Proposition and business plan who: • Creates, owns and maintains the model • Agrees methods and quality standards for the development of the model • Coordinates the related roles and capabilities • Facilitates knowledge transfer.
Business Owner	The person responsible for championing an idea from its first identification to the realisation of all its planned benefits. The Business Owner is additionally responsible for: • Owning and articulating the initiative vision, its purpose and value • Preparing and presenting the Bid for initial funding and full-funding • Ensuring that the impact of the initiative on the current operating model is assessed • Ensuring that the impact on the Target Operating Model is assessed and that results fit with the current architecture • Sponsoring the programme or project • Realising planned benefits and seeking additional benefit.

Role	Definition
Change Board	A panel of Executive Sponsors, chaired by a senior executive, who together are responsible for the realisation of benefits from the organisation's project portfolio. Responsibilities include:
	• Agreeing the balance and blend of the project portfolio
	• Authorising initiatives that will deliver the strategy and business plan
	• Approving initial and full funding of programmes, and projects
	• Monitoring status and progress, giving direction where appropriate
	• Monitoring the realisation of benefit from programmes, projects and continual improvement.
Change Office	The team who support the change planning and change delivery processes across the organisation. Responsibilities include:
	• Expediting the processing of ideas and coordination of facilitation services
	• Scheduling planned resources to programmes and projects
	• Supporting the inception, delivery and closure of programmes and projects
	• Monitoring the effective use and utilisation of resources
	• Maintaining policies, methods, standards, libraries and the Project Community Website
	• Gathering and collating management information
	• Tracking and expediting progress of programmes and projects
	• Preparing and circulating progress, status and performance reports
	• Managing the acquistion, storage and retrieval of knowledge.
Communication Manager	A person within a programme responsible to the Project Director for co-ordinating internal and external communications across a programme, ensuring that all communications are timely, and meet the quality standards of the organisation, with particular responsibility for:
	• Managing the Communication Plan
	• Preparing the content of each communication
	• Assuring the quality of communications through the approval processes
	• The effective delivery of internal and external communications
	• Measuring the effectiveness of communications.
Community of Practice	A cross-functional common interest group, comprising professional and occasional practitioners who have a job need to collaborate and share knowledge, expertise and experience for mutual benefit.
Customer Domain Manager	The project role of a domain manager implementing at least one deliverable that enables benefit realisation - responsibilities are:
	• Assessing the impact of the project on their domain
	• Agreeing the deliverables to be received, the requirements specification and the related quality standards
	• Committing specific resources of their own domain to the project
	• Empowering a Project Team Member to represent their own domain in the project
	• Ensuring that their own domain realises benefits from its participation in the project.

Role	Definition
Design Authority	A panel of domain architects, chaired by the Business Architect which:
	• Agrees the capbilities needed by the organisation in relation to the strategy and business plan
	• Identifies the benefits that will be generated from the Target Operating Model
	• Approves changes to the Target Operating Model.
Delivery Practice	An elite group of professional services practitioners employed within a fully funded function.
Domain Architect	A person responsible to the Programme Director for ensuring the conceptual integrity of a set of deliverables from a domain perspective - 'Domain' is replaced by the name of the domain represented, for example, Systems Architect, Technical Architect – whose responsibilities are:
	• Creating the conceptual model of the set of deliverables
	• Agreeing the development methods and quality standards needed to create or implement the set of deliverables
	• Co-ordinating the related roles and skills of the teams and individuals needed to create and approve or implement the set of deliverables
	• Facilitating knowledge transfer between the teams building or implementing the set of deliverables.
Domain Manager	A person responsible for the business performance of a domain, including:
	• Negotiating its budget, headcount, facilities, and performance targets
	• Managing the operation of the domain so that it achieves its performance targets.
Executive Sponsor	A member of a Change Board who is accountable for the strategy and business plan and takes responsibility for part of the project portfolio by:
	• Championing own initiatives
	• Advocating all approved programmes and projects
	• Selecting, appointing and empowering Business Owners
	• Driving realisation of planned benefits and seeking further benefit.
Financial Reviewer	A person within a programme, seconded from the finance function, responsible to the Programme Director for:
	• Providing objective and tactical financial advice and guidance
	• Providing support in relation to the organisation's financial systems
	• Conducting financial reviews of the programme and generation of its financial statements
	• Altering the business-as-usual budgets and performance targets to reflect the planned benefits
	• Measuring and reporting on the realisation of benefits.

Role	Definition
Head of Change	The person in an organisation responsible for: • Championing the change environment • Chairing the Change Board • Deciding the balance and blend of the project portfolio • Maintaining 'cabinet responsibility' within the Change Board • Resolving the inevitable conflicts that arise when deciding the relative merits of competing initiatives • Achieving needed benefits from discretionary spend.
Head of Demand	The person in an organisation responsible for: • Facilitating change decision making • Assessing new ideas and initiatives • Administering the discretionary spend budget • Co-ordinating benefit planning and realisation • Reporting progress and performance • Operating Value Management processes.
Head of Supply	The person in an organisation responsible for: • Recruiting and deploying capable and affordable resources to deliver change • Maintaining methods and the knowledge library • Coordinating learning and development • Sustaining the quality of change delivery • Operating the Resource Management processes, including rough-cut and finite capacity planning.
Programme Director	The person responsible to the Programme Sponsor for managing the external business, customer and major supplier relationships of the programme, whose responsibilities are: • Directing the programme in relation to realisation of the programme's vision • Creating a quality programme environment that enables the programme to succeed • Co-ordinating the management of internal and external communications • Guiding, supporting and, if necessary, deputising for the Programme Manager.
Programme Manager	The person responsible to the Programme Sponsor for the overall leadership, planning, organisation and management of the programme and its environment, ensuring the programme and each project is delivered within agreed targets so that planned benefits can be realised, whose responsibilities are: • Leading the Project Leaders • Planning what must be done • Organising the required resources • Managing the programme and its environment.

Role	Definition
Programme Office	A team within a programme, managed by the Programme Director, performing a similar function to a Change Office, responsible for: • Providing necessary services to the people involved in the programme • Maintaining a knowledge library • Gathering, collating and reporting Information.
Programme Sponsor	A person responsible to the Executive Board for championing the programme from idea to realisation of planned benefits, whose responsibilities are: • Owning and articulating the programme's vision and ensuring that it fits the current strategy and business plan, and is aligned with the Target Operating Model • Maintaining focus on the organisation's programme delivery aspirations and expectations • Managing the buy-in of the Programme Stakeholders • Supporting the Programme Director and Programme Manager
Programme Stakeholder	A person who has a vested interest in the outcome of the programme, who can influence the Programme Sponsor, whose cooperation is needed for project success, and whose responsibilities are: • Influencing the programme's vision, objectives and scope • Ensuring the views and requirements of the domains represented are taken into account • Agreeing the major changes that affect the domains represented • Advocate the programme to the people impacted • Monitor progress and performance • Identifying and validating benefits, and owning benefit realisation.
Programme Team	A team, chaired by the Programme Manager with membership including the Programme Director, Financial Reviewer, Domain Architects and Project Sponsors, accountable for: • Agreeing proposals and policies that will impact the programme • Effective inception of projects • Validating risks, issues and changes • Monitoring the progress of projects.
Project Leader	The person who is responsible for successful delivery of the project, working with the Project Partner. Responsibilities are: • Preparing project documentation • Planning the project with experts from customer and supplier domains • Organising required resources • Managing changes to the project • Leading the Project Team Members • Managing delivery and expectations • Taking action to ensure the success of the project.

Role	Definition
Project Partner	The person within a project who supports the Project Leader, complementing the Project Leader's knowledge, skill and experience. Responsibilities are: • Assisting the Project Leader in 'two man lift' work • Quality assuring the Project Leader's work • Supporting and, if necessary, deputising for, the Project Leader in day-to-day management of the project • Anticipating events and acting to ensure the success of the project.
Project Sponsor	The person responsible, through stakeholder management, for the success of the project. Responsibilities are: • Selecting, appointing, empowering and supporting the Project Leader and Project Partner • Identifying Project Stakeholders • Articulating and advocating the project vision • Deciding the project's objectives and scope.
Project Stakeholder	A manager of a large domain who has a vested interest in the outcome of the project, who can influence the Project Sponsor, whose cooperation is needed for project success and whose responsibilities are: • Representing the interests of own domain • Influencing the project's vision, objectives and scope • Identifying and validating benefits • Advocating the project.
Project Team	A team led by the Project Leader with members including the Project Partner and Project Team Members, that is accountable for: • Monitoring progress and agreeing remedial action • Progressing the project through inception, definition, planning, delivery and closure • Reviewing project risks, and agreeing proposed avoiding or mitigating actions and contingency plans • Formulating new issues • Reviewing change requests and recommending action.
Project Team Member	A person responsible for the completion of agreed work within a domain. Responsibilities are: • Ensuring the domain uses the agreed development methods and quality standards to create the agreed deliverables • Planning in detail the work of the domain • Negotiating target dates and resources with the Project Leader • Ensuring that the domain delivers as promised.
Relationship Owner	A person in business-as-usual who owns the relationship with an external supplier and is responsible for all dealings with the supplier.
Risk Owner	A subject matter expert in the area of risk who, having listened to the different points of view, is responsible for taking the final decision in respect of risk severity, agreeing mitigating actions, monitoring the risk and recommending use of the contingency plan.

Role	Definition
Steering Committee	A panel of selected stakeholders chaired by the Programme Sponsor with the Programme Director and Programme Manager as members, formed to validate, advocate, monitor and guide a programme in relation to strategic imperatives and realisation of benefits.
Subject Matter Expert	A person recognised as having exceptional specialist knowledge or skill, who can explain complex or specialist processes and entities in terms non-specialists can understand, and lead co-workers in the application of the processes or creation of the entities.
Supplier Domain Manager	The project role of a domain manager creating and deploying resources to make at least one deliverable - responsibilities are: <ul><li>Agreeing the deliverables to be created</li><li>Agreeing the development methods, the requirements specification and the related quality standards to be used for their creation</li><li>Committing specific resources of their own domain to the project</li><li>Empowering a Project Team Member to represent their own domain in the project.</li></ul>
Team Leader	The person within a team, empowered by the domain manager, responsible for: <ul><li>Operation of the team</li><li>Negotiation of its targets</li><li>Development of the team.</li></ul>
Team Member	A person within a team who is: <ul><li>Recruited and retained for personal knowledge, skills and experience</li><li>Empowered by the Team Leader</li><li>Accountable for work scheduled by the Team Leader.</li></ul>
Technical Architect	The person who is responsible for ensuring the conceptual integrity of the Target Operating Model from a technical perspective, and who: <ul><li>Creates and maintains the conceptual technical model</li><li>Agrees methods and quality standards for the development of the model</li><li>Coordinates the related roles and capabilities</li><li>Facilitates knowledge transfer.</li></ul>
Workstream Leader	A composite programme role, accountable to the Programme Manager, in support of the Executive Sponsor - a person who: <ul><li>Ensures initiatives are owned and championed from identification to realisation of planned benefits</li><li>Ensures projects are delivered within agreed targets</li><li>Ensures promised benefits are realised</li><li>Ensures progress and status are accurately reported</li><li>Leads Business Owners, Project Sponsors and Project Leaders, and performs these roles as required</li></ul>

Process Framework

The Verdandi framework of change management processes is illustrated below.

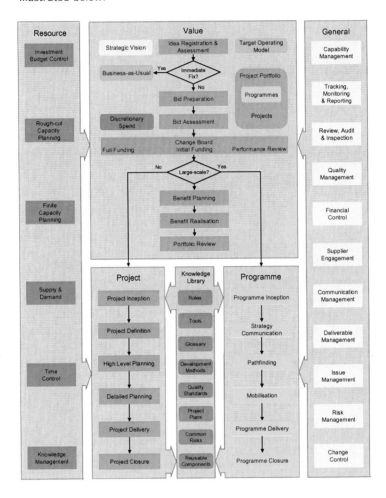

Figure 30: Process Framework

Value Management

Value Management is the policies, processes, standards and practices that enable the investment in initiatives to be governed effectively and ensure consistent worth to the organisation. Nine processes carry out Value Management:

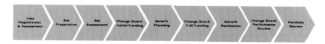

Figure 31: Value Management Processes

Idea Registration & Assessment

For each idea, the Business Owner completes an Initiative Sizing Matrix and an Initiative Scorecard

> *Idea Registration & Assessment is the process that:*
>
> - *Records the idea in the project portfolio*
> - *Sets out the idea as a partially completed Bid*
> - *Eliminates ideas that do not fit with the strategy.*

Although high level, these two documents allow ideas to be assessed, filtering out those for diversion to continual improvement and eliminating those that do not fit with the strategy. Where an idea complements or overlaps with another it is aggregated.

Unless enabling benefits elsewhere, ideas offering no prospect of value are terminated at this point. The remaining ideas are advanced to the next stage.

Bid Preparation

> *Bid Preparation is process in which a **Bid** for resources, including the **Investment Appraisal**, is completed based on expert opinion and judgement rather than detailed analysis.*

The Bid describes the idea in commercial and financial terms so that it can be assessed as a potential initiative.

Bid Assessment

> **Bid Assessment is the process in which a Bid is assessed in its own right and in relation to the entire project portfolio.**

The entire project portfolio must be taken into account when ranking new initiatives against the strategic imperatives to decide the optimum-value sequence of delivery, subject to known interdependencies, as well as financial and manpower affordability.

The Resource Management processes Investment Budget Control and Rough-cut Capacity Planning are used to assess financial and manpower affordability.

At this point, Bids will either be:

- Accepted and given the green light to proceed

- Deferred until the time is right to proceed

- Referred for clarification

- Declined - stopped with immediate effect.

The Change Board meets on a regular basis to make these decisions and discuss the progress of existing and new initiatives in the project portfolio.

Change Board - Initial Funding

> **Change Board - Initial funding is the process that:**
>
> - **Approves, defers or rejects initiatives for advancement as programmes and projects in the context of the entire project portfolio.**
>
> - **Awards initial funding to projects for necessary research, definition and planning; sufficient for a definitive Cost Benefit Analysis or full Business Case to be created.**

Investment Budget Control and Rough-cut Capacity Planning are used to assess affordability.

If the initiative is awarded initial funding, then, depending on the size and complexity, it will be incepted as either a programme or project.

Benefit Planning

Benefit Planning is the process that:

- **Links anticipated benefits through project or programme objectives to the company's strategic imperatives**

- **Identifies the specific changes that will enable benefit realisation**

- **Makes the realisation of each benefit the responsibility of a named Benefit Owner.**

Benefit Planning occurs between the 'Project Definition' and 'High Level Planning' processes and during the Programme Management 'Pathfinding' process. The role of the Benefit Owner is key to this process.

Change Board – Full Funding

Change Board – Full funding is the process that:

- **Approves, defers or rejects projects and programmes for delivery on the basis of a defensible business case in the context of the entire project portfolio**

- **Adjusts business-as-usual budgets, key performance indicators and personal targets of Benefit Owners on the basis of the Benefit Plan.**

The Resource Management processes Investment Budget Control, Rough-cut Capacity Planning and Finite Capacity Planning are used in assessing affordability.

If the project or programme is awarded full funding then it will be authorised to proceed to the 'Project Delivery' process or the programme management 'Mobilisation' process.

Benefit Realisation

Benefit Realisation is the process by which Executive Sponsors, Business Owners and Benefit Owners take full advantage of every opportunity to realise value.

Benefit realisation is a continuing task, starting after the first deliverables are handed over to business-as-usual.

Change Board - Performance Review

> **Change Board – Performance Review is the process that:**
>
> - **Reviews the progress of programmes and projects towards complete delivery and benefit realisation**
>
> - **Agrees remedial actions for projects and programmes for which current slippage can be recovered**

Large-scale projects and programmes are reviewed at stages, typically every 90 days. If a project is indicating slippage, the corresponding issues are reviewed. Those with irrecoverable slippage or where the promised benefits cannot be realised may be re-scoped or terminated.

Portfolio Review

> **Portfolio Review is the process that makes a periodic review of the entire project portfolio to ensure that projects and programmes will deliver the organisation's strategy and business plan.**

From time to time a periodic review of the Initiative Scorecard and the entire project portfolio is crucial to ensure that programmes and projects are making a coherent contribution to the achievement of the organisation's strategy and business plan.

Value Management ensures that executives retain their responsibility for the success of their business-as-usual operation whilst working within a governed environment that is consistent across the organisation.

Resource Management

Resource Management is the policies, processes, standards and practices that enable the resources of an organisation to be optimally deployed so that more can be accomplished with less resource. Six processes carry out Resource Management.

Figure 32: Resource Management Processes

Investment Budget Control

> **Investment Budget Control is the process that:**
>
> - **Determines the size and deployment of the discretionary spend**
>
> - **Monitors the allocation over time of spend to programmes and projects**
>
> - **Ensures that approval is given only to programmes and projects that are affordable and viable.**

The investment budget provides both initial and full funding to programmes and projects. By this approach, it is possible to launch more programmes and projects that can be afforded – the least beneficial are 'weeded out' and funding granted only to 'sure-fire winners'.

Rough-cut Capacity Planning

> **Rough-cut Capacity Planning is the process which monitors people's availability for deployment to business-as-usual and initiative-related work, to ensure that:**
>
> - **Approval is not given to more initiatives than can be delivered with the resources available**
>
> - **'Hot spots' in the critical resource centres and applications of the business are identified.**

Provides the organisation with clear answer to the questions: "Do we have roughly enough resources to deliver that which is being asked of us?" and "Can the organisation reasonably absorb the changes we are planning to make?"

It is often impractical or unaffordable to monitor the availability of everything. By focusing on 'hard to obtain' resources effective alternatives can be considered.

It requires little effort and timely resolution of issues circumvents the resource and capacity 'bankruptcy' problems that can so easily de-rail timely realisation of benefits.

Finite Capacity Planning

Finite Capacity Planning is the process that predicts, in detail, the future demand for resources – it identifies pinchpoints in the availability of infrastructure and people with key skills or subject matter expertise, and either increases capacity or reschedules work around the constraint.

A pinchpoint is a current or imminent shortage of facilities or of people with key skills or subject matter expertise.

Supply & Demand

Supply & Demand is the process that satisfies the organisation's need for capable people by managing the acquisition and deployment of people to specific roles.

Otherwise excellent projects can be ruined if the wrong people are assigned to roles. Success requires 'the right people, with the right knowledge, skills and experience, in the right place at the right time.'

Supply & Demand manages available resources to maximise the contribution the organisation's people can make.

Time Control

Time Control is the process that monitors the actual against planned use of manpower, person by person, to account for resource utilisation and enable invoices from external suppliers and cross-charges from internal suppliers to be verified.

Time Control prevents unconscious squandering of resources and identifies high and low performers. When work involves suppliers working to 'time and materials' contracts, Time Control is essential.

Knowledge Management

> **Knowledge Management is the process that captures and distils knowledge, and re-usable components from programmes and projects and makes it easily accessible for re-use.**

When disorganised, the greater the knowledge, the greater the confusion. Organising the knowledge and making it easily accessible, on-demand to the people who need it via the organisation's intranet is a key driver of high performance.

Knowledge Management deals with the re-usable components acquired by programmes - that's mundane – creating a culture of people taking time to codify the knowledge they carry in their heads and store it so that others can benefit - that's special - and too valuable to lose.

Programme Management

Programme Management is the agile and adaptable application of a set of processes to define, plan and deliver large-scale, beneficial change to an organisation. Six processes carry out Programme Management.

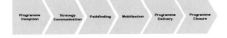

Figure 33: Programme Management Processes

Programme Inception

> *Programme Inception is the process that launches the programme successfully and:*
>
> - *Puts in place key role holders*
>
> - *Agrees the programme management approach and infrastructure.*

Programme Inception lays the foundations of the programme by agreeing its shape. This includes identifying the Programme Stakeholders and the members of the Steering Committee, agreeing key development methods, deciding the administrative and management structures including governance functions devolved to the programme.

Strategy Communication

> *Strategy Communication is the process that articulates the vision and strategy to be implemented by the programme to:*
>
> - *Gain organisation focus and buy-in*
>
> - *Enable identification of the projects required*
>
> - *Create a clear context for the realisation of benefits.*

The preferred method for communicating strategy for a programme is a Programme Vision document. It enables those who are impacted by the programme, such as suppliers or customers, to understand the whole context of what is intended and what they have to do. The Programme Vision is an input to Benefit Planning.

Pathfinding

> **Pathfinding is the process that:**
>
> - **Establishes the feasibility and viability of the programme**
> - **Defines its scope and objectives in parallel with the Benefit Planning process**
> - **Segments the programme into its constituent projects and creates its Implementation Schedule**
> - **Plans the programme organisation structure**
> - **Develops the full Business Case.**

Pathfinding is a major planning process in programme management. If it is done fully and well, the journey will be successful. If skimped, costs and timescales may spiral and the programme run out of control.

Mobilisation

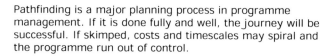

> **Mobilisation is the process that:**
>
> - **Organises the resources required to deliver the programme**
> - **Formally agrees all related contracts and service level agreements**
> - **Incepts the projects that constitute the programme.**

Mobilisation is the bridge between planning and delivery.

Programme Delivery

> **Programme Delivery is the process that:**
>
> - **Monitors, controls and reports progress on the programme and its constituent projects**
> - **Ensures the successful delivery of the programme and its constituent projects**
> - **Focuses attention on benefit realisation usually through a benefit realisation project.**

As each project starts and delivers, so the programme will progress, consuming time and resources. The monitoring, controlling and reporting the progress and status of this spend will be at the forefront of the minds of those providing the funding, as they check to make sure that their return on investment is achieved in the timeframe agreed. Special attention therefore must be paid to benefit realisation.

Programme Closure

Programme Closure is the process that:

- **Disengages the people assigned to the programme**
- **Archives re-usable knowledge in the knowledge library**
- **Formally ends all work and expenditure on the programme.**

Much will have been learned during a programme; it is important that this is not lost. Many people will have contributed to the success – they should be rewarded accordingly and success celebrated!

Processes

The following table lists the processes used within change management and the capability they fall within.

Strategy & General	Value Management	Resource Management	Project Management	Programme Management

Process	Definition
Benefit Planning	The process that: • Links anticipated benefits through programme or project objectives to the company's strategic imperatives • Identifies the specific changes that will enable benefit realisation • Makes the realisation of each benefit the responsibility of a named Benefit Owner.
Benefit Realisation	The process by which Executive Sponsors, Business Owners and Benefit Owners take full advantage of every opportunity to realise value.
Bid Assessment	The process in which a Bid is assessed in its own right and in relation to the entire project portfolio.
Bid Preparation	The process in which a Bid for resources, including the Investment Appraisal, is completed based on expert opinion and judgement rather than detailed analysis.
Capability Management	The process by which: • The organisation's required capabilities are developed and maintained within the Target Operating Model to align with the strategy • The strategic vision is communicated to the people responsible for and impacted by implementation • Work to create the capabilities is prioritised and initiated • Achievement of capabilities in the Target Operating Model and realisation of associated benefits as a result of implementing planned initiatives is reported.
Change Board - Full Funding	The process that: • Approves, defers or rejects projects and programmes for delivery on the basis of a defensible Cost Benefit Analysis or Business Case in the context of the entire project portfolio • Adjusts business-as-usual budgets, key performance indicators, and personal targets of Benefit Owners on the basis of the Benefit Plan.
Change Board - Initial Funding	The process that: • Approves, defers or rejects initiatives for advancement as programmes and projects in the context of the entire project portfolio • Awards initial funding to approved projects for necessary research, definition and delivery planning; sufficient for a definitive Cost Benefit Analysis or Business Case to be created.

Strategy & General	Value Management	**Resource Management**	Project Management	Programme Management

Process	Definition

Change Board - Performance Review
The process that:
- Reviews the progress of programmes and projects towards complete delivery and benefit realisation
- Agrees remedial actions for programmes and projects for which current slippage can be recovered
- Re-scopes, re-schedules, or terminates programmes and projects that are irrecoverably slipping.

Change Control
The process by which requests for change to any aspect of a project are validated, assessed, rejected or authorised, implemented or deferred.

Communication Management
The process by which the Communication Plan of a programme or project is planned, designed and delivered.

Deliverable Management
The process by which deliverables are created, tested and operationally proven so that quality is assured.

Detailed Planning
The process which breaks the project down to a level of detail at which:
- Accurate estimates of cost, manpower and time can be made
- The completion of specific activities can be made the responsibility of named Project Team Members
- Risks can be managed
- The Project Leader can be confident in the ability of the project team to deliver successfully.

Financial Control
The process by which:
- Necessary money is made available to programmes and projects from the investment budget at the right time
- Expenditure is approved in line with the organisation's policy and procedures
- Benefit realisation is measured and reflected in changes to both organisational and personal performance targets.

Finite Capacity Planning
The process that predicts, in detail, the future demand for specific skilled resources, identifies pinchpoints in the availability of infrastructure and people with key skills and expertise, and either increases capacity or reschedules work around the constraint.

High Level Planning
The process that:
- Establishes the development methods, deliverables, specicfications, quality standards and dependencies within a project
- Shows in outline how the project will be conducted and achieved
- Creates a revised Cost Benefit Analysis for the project.

Idea Registration & Assessment
The process that:
- Records the idea in the project portfolio
- Sets out the idea as a partially completed Bid
- Eliminates ideas that do not fit with the strategy.

© Verdandi Limited 1984-2010

Strategy & General	Value Management	**Resource Management**	Project Management	Programme Management

Process	Definition
Investment Budget Control	The process that: • Determines the size and deployment of the discretionary spend • Monitors the allocation over time of spend to programmes and projects • Ensures that approval is given only to programmes and projects that are affordable and viable.
Issue Management	The process by which an identified issue is recorded and escalated to a level at which it can be resolved.
Knowledge Management	The process that captures and distils knowledge, and re-usable components from programmes and projects and makes it easily accessible for re-use.
Mobilisation	The process that: • Organises the resources required to deliver the programme • Formally agrees all related contracts and service level agreements • Incepts the projects that constitute the programme.
Pathfinding	The process that: • Establishes the feasibility and viability of the programme • Defines its scope and objectives in parallel with the Benefit Planning process • Segments the programme into its constituent projects • Determines dependencies between key deliverables • Creates the Implementation Schedule • Plans the programme organisation structure • Develops the Business Case.
Portfolio Review	The process that makes a periodic review of the entire project portfolio to ensure that current programmes and projects will deliver the organisation's strategy and business plan.
Programme Closure	The process that: • Disengages the people assigned to the programme • Archives re-usable knowledge in the knowledge library • Formally ends all work and expenditure on the programme.
Programme Delivery	The process that: • Monitors, controls and reports progress on the programme and its constituent projects • Ensures the successful delivery of the programme and its constituent projects • Focuses attention on benefit realisation usually through a benefit realiosation project.
Programme Inception	The process that launches the programme successfully and: • Puts in place key role holders • Agrees the programme management approach and infrastructure.

Strategy & General	Value Management	**Resource Management**	Project Management	Programme Management

Process	Definition

⬧ Project Closure — The process that:

- Disengages the people assigned to the project
- Archives re-usable knowledge in the knowledge library
- Formally ends all work and expenditure on the project.

⬧ Project Definition — The process that:

- Establishes a common, balanced and agreed view of what has to be done and by when
- Identifies the project objectives and scope, key deliverables and expectations
- Clarifies the scope, constraints and deadline.

⬧ Project Delivery — The process that manages the promises made by Project Team Members and applies agreed tracking, monitoring, and reporting processes to ensure the project is delivered according to plan.

⬧ Project Inception — The process that launches the project successfully and:

- Puts in place key role holders
- Agrees the project management approach and infrastructure.

⬦ Quality Management — The process that is used to validate the adequacy, continually improve and adapt, or acquire new quality standards and development methods, where necessary.

⬦ Review, Audit & Inspection — The process that is used to examine the conduct, probity and the compliance of programmes and projects.

⬦ Risk Management — The process of making the risks inherent in a project explicit, and increasing the likelihood of success by:

- Assessing the risks to the outcome of the project
- Evaluating the probability and impact
- Determining mitigating actions
- Making contingency plans for high and unacceptable risks
- Seeking ways of avoiding risks
- Monitoring and re-assessing risks at agreed intervals.

✦ Rough-cut Capacity Planning — The process that monitors people's availability for deployment to business-as-usual and initiative-related work, to ensure that:

- Approval is not given to more initiatives than can be delivered with the resources available
- 'Hot spots' in the critical resource centres and the applications of the business are identified.

⬦ Strategy Acceleration — The process by which:

- Gaps in capability and thinking are identified
- Organisational focus and buy-in is achieved
- Projects that will deliver the strategy and business plan are identified
- A clear context is created for the planning and realisation of benefits.

Strategy & General	Value Management	**Resource Management**	Project Management	Programme Management

Process	Definition
Strategy Communication	The process that articulates the vision and strategy to be implemented by the programme to:

- Gain organisation focus and buy-in
- Enable identification of the projects required
- Create a clear context for the realisation of benefits.

Supplier Engagement	The process by which suppliers are selected, evaluated and formally appointed.
Supply & Demand	The process that satisfies the organisation's need for adequate numbers of capable people by:

- Planning the capabilities, key competencies, skills needed by the organisation to enable recruitment
- Assessing and testing leadership skills and key competencies against required capabilities and selecting the best people at the right price
- Engaging people in accordance with a robust due diligence process that delivers clear contractual terms
- Equipping people for their intended roles and taking them through an induction process
- Ensuring that people receive appropriate training and development for their intended roles
- Allocating and deploying people to specific roles with a clear role description and terms of reference
- De-allocating people from roles and either re-deploying them to new roles or exiting them from the organisation in accordance with their contact of employment.

Time Control	The process that monitors the actual against planned use of manpower, person by person, to account for resource utilisation and enable invoices from external suppliers and cross-charges from internal suppliers to be validated.
Tracking, Monitoring & Reporting	The process by which information is gathered, collated and reported about the status and progress of programmes and projects.

Tools

The following table lists tools used within change management, indicating the area of capability in which use each tool is mainly used.

Tool	Definition	Strategy Acceleration	Value Management	Resource Management	Project Management	Programme Management
Assumption Log	The inventory of assumptions current in a programme or project.					•
Benefit Plan	The timetable and responsibilities for the realisation of the benefits of an initiative.		•			
Benefit Report	The originally planned, currently planned and actual realisation of benefits of an initiative.		•			
Benefit Schedule	A timetable of all initiatives, grouped into programmes and related families within a project portfolio, it is used to show interdependencies and the anticipated benefits (see Integrated Plan).					•
Benefit Structure	A tool used to increase the explicitness of identified benefits.		•			
Bid	The simple business case for an initiative to receive initial funding or full-funding presented by the Executive Sponsor and Business Owner to the Change Board, it includes: • Investment Appraisal • Initiative Sizing Matrix • Initiative Scorecard • Initiative Details • Value Analysis • Cost Benefit Analysis.		•			
Business Case	The justification of an investment and the allocation of sufficient resources, so that its worth can be reviewed in the context of strategy and impact on the organisation – it contains a Cost Benefit Analysis and Investment Appraisal.		•			
Capacity Plan	A plan that shows the current utilisation, forecast utilisation, and ultimate capacity of the organisations resources and assets – highlighting shortfalls and excesses.					•
Change Board Agenda	A schedule of the topics to be addressed at each Change Board meeting.			•		
Change Log	The definitive record of changes to any aspect of the project.				•	
Change Management Policy	Rulings that apply across the organisation for the management of initiatives and acquisition and deployment of human, financial, infrastructure and knowledge resources – telling you what you can do.			•		
Commitment Analysis	A tool used to evaluate the commitment of Benefit Owners to realising benefits identified in the Benefit Plan.		•			

	Strategy Acceleration	Value Management	Resource Management	Project Management	Programme Management
Tool	**Definition**				**Capability**
Communication Plan	A schedule of timely communications, that uses a variety of channels and media to ensure people understand the reasons for change, how it will be implemented, and how it will impact them personally or the groups they represent.				◦
Contact List	A directory of people undertaking specific roles on a project or programme.				◦
Competency Assessment Profile	The findings of an analytical assessment of the key competencies, skills, style, knowledge and experience of a person for a particular role.			◦	
Continuity Plan	A plan that can be used to successfully re-create an environment in the event of a disaster.				◦
Cost Benefit Analysis	The benefits, costs and manpower of an initiative indicating margins of error, and set out to demonstrate the measurable value (see Bid).				◦
Cost Control	The originally planned, currently planned, and actual costs incurred by a project.				◦
Cost Estimate	A schedule of expected expenditure by expense type and by phase and task of a project.				◦
Cost Schedule	A timetable of all initiatives, grouped into programmes and related families within a project portfolio, it is used to show interdependencies and the anticipated costs (see Integrated Plan).			◦	
Critical Resource Schedule	A timetable of all initiatives, grouped into programmes and related families within a project portfolio, it is used to show interdependencies and the anticipated critical resources (see Integrated Plan).			◦	
Critical Success Factor Log	The inventory of critical success factors current in a programme or project.				◦
Customer Review	The report of a customer satisfaction survey.				◦
Definition Interview Notes	Used to agree the individual views and opinions of the sponsor and each of the stakeholders.				◦
Deliverable Approval	The formal record of the acceptance of a deliverable by at least one domain manager and by the Programme or Project Sponsor for a key deliverable.				◦
Deliverable Log	The definitive record of all the deliverables that will be produced by a project, with key deliverables flagged for reporting purposes.				◦
Dependency Analysis	A chart used to: • Determine the dependencies between key deliverables • Validate the logical sequence of production • Confirm the achievability of the deadlines • Indicate when benefit realisation will be triggered.				◦

	Strategy Acceleration	Value Management	Resource Management	Project Management	Programme Management
Tool	**Definition**				**Capability**
Domain Matrix	Used in the analysis of impact of the project on the current internal and external domains of the organisation.				✓
Due Activities Report	Those activities in the Task & Activity List, the target dates of which are earlier than a specific date, used to expedite their completion.				✓
End of Assignment Report	An assessment of the Project Leader's performance on the project by the Business Owner.				✓
Forecast Manpower	Used in to show the accumulated manpower projected to be used on current and planned initiatives over time, compared to the understood capacity threshold.				✓
Forecast Manpower by Domain	Used in to show the accumulated manpower projected to be used on current and planned initiatives over time, in critical resource centres, compared to the understood capacity threshold.				✓
Glossary of Terms	A defined list of non-dictionary, business and technical terms and abbreviations relating to the subject matter of a programme or project, used to help people joining the programme or project to understand and participate more effectively.				✓
Heat Map	A chart of accumulated impacts of the project portfolio on the capabilities, domains and applications of an organisation, at given time periods, indicating the 'hot spots'.				✓
Initiative Details	Describes the work as currently understood; and is the Project Leader's starting point (see Bid).				✓
Initiative Scorecard	Used to assess the potential contribution that an initiative will make to the achievement of the strategy and business plan (see Bid).				✓
Initiative Sizing Matrix	Used to assess the complexity and the business risk of an initiative (see Bid).				✓
Implementation Schedule	A timetable of projects, grouped into families of projects within a portfolio, it is used to show interdependencies and manpower.				✓
Integrated Plan	A timetable of all initiatives, grouped into programmes and related families within a project portfolio, it is used to show interdependencies and cascaded to show the anticipated manpower, costs, and benefits – it includes:				✓
Inventory Analysis	Used in the analysis of a programme's impact on the current assets of an organisation.				✓
Investment Appraisal	Used to measure the commercial worth of an initiative against specific investment criteria determined by the organisation (see Bid).				✓

For Integrated Plan:

- Resource Schedule

- Critical Resource Schedule

- Cost Schedule

- Benefit Schedule

	Strategy Acceleration	Value Management	Resource Management	Project Management	Programme Management
Tool	**Definition**				**Capability**
Investment Budget Allocation	The accumulated discretionary spend allocated to current and planned programmes and projects over time, compared to the monthly investment threshold.				•
Issue List	Used for broadcasting key decisions and bringing issues for which resolutions have not been provided in a timely manner to the attention of the Project Sponsor, Steering Committee, and Change Board.				•
Issue Log	The definitive record and audit trail of identified, escalated and resolved issues on a project.				•
Key Deliverable Report	A report of the planned, forecast and actual dates for completion of key deliverables.				•
Manpower Control	A report of the variance between estimated and actual manpower used on a project.				•
Manpower Estimate	A schedule of expected use of manpower by domain and skill and by phase and task of a project.				•
Manpower Schedule	A rough-cut time related estimate, used within a given domain to compare the manpower required to complete known project related and business-as-usual work with the manpower available to do work, over an agreed planning horizon, highlighting shortfalls and surpluses.				•
Master Project Definition	The 'contract' between the Programme Manager and Programme Sponsor for the management of the programme.				•
Meeting & Reporting Schedule	Used to plan and control the timing and attendance of meeting and the timing and circulation of reports of a project.				•
Meeting Minutes	Used in the recording of actions and decisions from formal programme and project meetings.				•
Milestone Report	A report of the planned, forecast and actual dates for completion of the phases of a project.				•
Minute-by-Minute Schedule	A timed plan used to co-ordinate the completion of a number of inter-related activities within a project on a very detailed time and sequence critical basis.				•
Overall Programme Definition	The 'contract' between the Programme Sponsor and Programme Manager for the completion of the programme that sets out its agreed objectives and scope, its key deliverables, assumptions, constraints and de-commit criteria.				•
Phase Plan	A list of the phases of a project.				•
Portfolio Business Case	Shows the costs and benefits of all current initiatives over five years, used to prove that the project portfolio is commercially viable.				•
Portfolio Consolidation	Captures all the relevant Bid information on the project portfolio database so that it can be sorted and reported.				•
Post-Programme Review	The report of a post-programme review which shows that the programme was successful or not.				•

	Strategy Acceleration	Value Management	**Resource Management**	Project Management	Programme Management
Tool	Definition				Capability
Post-Project Review	The report of a post-project review which shows that the project was successful or not.				⟡
Precedence Diagram	A schematic of a project showing the dependencies between its phases, used to drive the negotiation of delivery promises.				⟡
Programme Binder	A physical book set out in standard sections and containing the key programme documents, used by the Programme Manager as a handy reference and to evidence to audiences the programme status.				⟡
Programme Budget	A schedule of expected expenditure by expense type of a programme.				⟡
Programme Meeting Agenda	The standard agenda of a meeting of the Programme Team.				⟡
Programme Organisation Structure	Used to show the reporting between programme roles.				⟡
Programme Policy	The rulings that describe 'How we do things around here' within the programme's environment including: • Its organisation design, roles, responsibilities and reporting lines • The development methods to be used for the construction of key deliverables and agreed guidelines for application • The processes to be used for value, resource, programme and project management.				⟡
Programme Vision	See Strategic Vision.				⟡
Progress Report	A summary of the achievement against all key performance criteria for the Executive Sponsor and Change Board used instead of individual reports.			⟡	
Project Binder	A physical book organised in standard sections and containing the key project documents, used by the Project Leader as a handy reference and to evidence to different audiences the status of the project.			⟡	
Project Definition	The 'contract' between the Project Sponsor and Project Leader for the completion of the project setting out its objectives and scope, key deliverables, assumptions and constraints.			⟡	
Project Meeting Agenda	The standard agenda of a meeting of the Project Leader, Project Partner and Project Team Members.			⟡	
Project Organisation Structure	Used to show the reporting between project roles.			⟡	
Project Start Template	A standard list of all the recommended tasks and activities that a Project Leader should consider in defining, planning, delivering, reviewing and closing a project.			⟡	

Strategy Acceleration	Value Management	Resource Management	Project Management	Programme Management

Tool	Definition	Capability
Realisation Analysis	A charting technique used to link the organisation's strategic imperatives to the objectives from the Project Definition and the benefits from the Cost Benefit Analysis, so as to identify the necessary: • Changes required to enable benefit realisation • Enablers that make change possible • Components of enablers.	•
Requirements Specification	The functionality, usability and acceptability that the customer expects from the implementation and subsequent operation of a deliverable.	•
Resource Schedule	A timetable of all initiatives, grouped into programmes and related families within a project portfolio, it is used to show interdependencies and the anticipated manpower resources (see Integrated Plan).	•
Risk Log	The definitive record of risks throughout the life of a programme or project.	•
Risk Return Matrix	Used to show the financial worth and spread of business risk that initiatives making up the project portfolio have.	•
Role Profile	Used to identify the competencies, skills and knowledge needed of suitable candidates.	•
Role Reporting Structure	A temporary organisation structure showing the reporting relationships between roles within a programme.	•
Rough-cut Estimate	A non-binding but logically determined amount of manpower, money or time needed for the completion of a project.	•
Shaping Interview Notes	Used to confirm the view of the Programme Sponsor of the shape of the programme or the Project Sponsor of the shape of the project.	•
Skill Schedule	A timetable that lists the total number of man-days effort required, by skill type and experience level, within a domain or team.	•
Stage Review	Used to record the actions and decisions from a Stage Review of a programme or large-scale project.	•
Stakeholder Analysis	Used to evaluate the commitment of the people who have the power to influence the outcome of a programme or project to the changes that might be needed.	•
Steering Committee Agenda	The standard agenda of a meeting of the Steering Committee.	•
Strategic Alignment	Used to show the contribution that initiatives within the project portfolio will make to the strategy and the strategic imperatives.	•
Strategic Impact – External View	Used to show the spread of impact that initiatives making up the project portfolio will have on the customer proposition and customer service.	•

	Value Management	**Resource Management**		Programme Management
Strategy Acceleration			Project Management	

Tool	Definition	Capability
Strategic Impact – Internal View	Used to show the spread of impact that initiatives making up the project portfolio will have on the internal operations of the organisation.	✓
Strategic Impact Matrix	Used to show the combined impact that initiatives making up the project portfolio will have on the internal and external operations of the organisation.	✓
Strategic Vision	Used to form the links between the strategy, Customer Value Proposition and Target Operating Model, and communicate the needed outcomes so that people impacted can support the change and participate more effectively in the development of the business.	✓
Supplier Review	Used to record the actions and decisions from a supplier review.	✓
Task & Activity List	The phases, tasks and activities of a project set out to show in detail how the project will be managed and how each of the deliverables will be created.	✓
Terms of Reference	The definition of the objectives and scope of a complex task to be completed within business-as-usual.	✓
Timesheet	A record of the time a person has spent on different categories of work, to account for manpower utilisation and enable invoices from external suppliers and cross-charges from internal suppliers to be verified.	✓
Timesheet Analysis by Person	An analysis of the time people have spent on work, it is used by the Project Leader to evidence that value has been achieved before authorising payment to suppliers.	✓
Timesheet Analysis by Project	An analysis of the time people have spent on work, it is used by the Project Leader to authorise re-charge of the services to the customer.	✓
Tracking Report	A record of the progress of ideas from registration to benefit realisation through agreed checkpoints.	✓
Value Analysis	Identifies the sensitivities to establish the chance of higher or lower benefit (see Bid).	✓
Work Schedule	A snapshot view of person's work-plan detailing all commitments to administration, business-as-usual and project-related activities over a given time period.	✓

Value Toolkit

The following table lists the value tools and shows the Value Management processes in which they are used, indicating applicability to organisation size and the typical sequence in which they might be deployed.

Legend for Recommended Frequency / Organisation Size: O = Optional, M = Mandatory, R = Recommended.

Idea Registration & Assessment	Bid Preparation	Bid Assessment	Change Board – Initial Funding	Benefit Planning	Change Board – Full Funding	Benefit Realisation	Change Board – Performance Review	Tool	Recommended Frequency	Small	Moderate	Large
				5				Benefit Plan	Version Control	M	M	M
						8		Benefit Report	Version Control	M	M	M
				4				Benefit Structure	Version Control	R	R	R
2								Bid*	Version Control	M	M	M
		10						Change Board Agenda	Version Control	M	M	M
		8						Change Management Policy	Version Control	R	R	R
				6				Commitment Analysis	Version Control	R	R	R
		16						Forecast Manpower	Event Driven	O	R	R
		17						Forecast Manpower by Domain	Event Driven	O	R	R
		18						Portfolio Business Case	Event Driven	O	R	R
		9						Portfolio Consolidation	Event Driven	O	R	R
				3				Realisation Analysis	Version Control	R	R	R
		15						Risk Return Matrix	Event Driven	O	R	R
							7	Stage Review	Version Control	O	O	O
		11						Strategic Alignment	Event Driven	O	R	R
		13						Strategic Impact – External View	Event Driven	O	R	R
		12						Strategic Impact – Internal View	Event Driven	O	R	R
		14						Strategic Impact Matrix	Event Driven	O	R	R
1								Terms of Reference	Event Driven	O	O	O

*Bid includes an Investment Appraisal, an Initiative Sizing Matrix, an Initiative Scorecard the Initiative Details, a Value Analysis and a Cost Benefit Analysis. Only the Initiative Details and Cost Benefit Analysis are mandatory. The Cost Benefit Analysis is maintained through the project lifecycle.

Resource Toolkit

The following table lists the resource tools and shows the Resource Management processes in which they are used, indicating applicability to organisation size and the typical sequence in which they might be deployed.

Investment Budget Control	Rough-cut Capacity Planning	Finite Capacity Planning	Supply & Demand	Time Control	Knowledge Management	Tool	Recommended Frequency (O = Optional, M = Mandatory, R = Recommended)	Small	Moderate	Large
	7					Benefit Schedule *	Event Driven	M	M	M
		10				Capacity Plan	Event Driven	O	R	M
			13			Competency Assessment Profile	As required	O	R	R
	6					Cost Schedule *	Event Driven	M	M	M
	5					Critical Resource Schedule *	Event Driven	O	R	R
			15			End of Assignment Report	Event Driven	O	R	R
	9					Heat Map	Event Driven	O	R	R
	3					Integrated Plan	Event Driven	M	M	M
1						Investment Budget Allocation	Event Driven	M	M	M
	2					Manpower Schedule	Event Driven	O	R	R
	4					Resource Schedule *	Event Driven	M	M	M
			12			Role Profile	As Required	M	M	M
		11				Skill Schedule	Event Driven	O	R	R
				16		Timesheet	Daily	O	O	O
				17		Timesheet Analysis by Person	Monthly	O	O	O
				18		Timesheet Analysis by Project	Monthly	O	O	O
	8					Tracking Report	Event Driven	O	R	R
			14			Work Schedule	As required	O	O	O

* These together form the Integrated Plan

Programme Toolkit

The following table lists the programme tools and shows the Programme Management processes in which they are used, indicating applicability to programme size and recommended sequence of document production.

A programme's master project will use Project Toolkit™.

If governance is performed within the programme, the programme will use the Value and Resource Toolkits.

Programme Inception	Strategy Communication	Pathfinding	Mobilisation	Programme Delivery	Programme Closure	Tool	Recommended Frequency O = Optional M = Mandatory R = Recommended	Moderate	Complex	Very Complex
		7				Business Case	Version Control	O	R	R
				16		Continuity Plan	Version Control	O	R	R
		4				Definition Interview Notes	Version Control	M	M	M
		6				Dependency Analysis	Version Control	O	R	M
			15			Implementation Schedule	Version Control	R	M	M
			14			Inventory Analysis	Version Control	O	O	O
			11			Master Project Definition	Version Control	R	M	M
		5				Overall Programme Definition	Version Control	M	M	M
					17	Post-Programme Review	Version Control	R	R	R
1						Programme Binder	Version Control	O	O	O
		8				Programme Budget	Version Control	R	R	R
			12			Programme Meeting Agenda	Monthly	R	R	R
			9			Programme Organisation Structure	Version Control	R	R	M
			13			Programme Policy	Version Control	R	R	R
	3					Programme Vision	Version Control	O	R	M
			10			Role Reporting Structure	Version Control	O	O	O
	2					Steering Committee Agenda	Monthly	R	M	M

Project Toolkit

The following table lists the project tools and shows the Project
Management processes in which they are used, indicating
applicability to project size and recommended sequence of
document production.

Project Management Process					Tool	Recommended Frequency O = Optional M = Mandatory R = Recommended	Project Size	
Project Inception	Project Definition	High Level Planning	Detailed Planning	Project Delivery	Project Closure		Smaller	Larger
	9					Assumption Log	Version Control	O	O
				30		Change Log	As required	R	R
		21				Communication Plan	Version Control	O	R
		14				Contact List	Version Control	O	O
2						Cost Benefit Analysis (part of Bid)	Version Control	M	M
				34		Cost Control	Weekly	O	R
			29			Cost Estimate	Version Control	O	R
	10					Critical Success Factor Log	Version Control	O	O
					39	Customer Review	As required	O	O
	6					Definition Interview Notes	Version Control	R	R
				37		Deliverable Approval	As required	O	R
		17				Deliverable Log	Version Control	M	M
		13				Domain Matrix	Version Control	O	R
				36		Due Activities Report	Weekly	O	O
		16				Glossary of Terms	Version Control	O	O
1						Initiative Details (part of Bid)	Version Control	R	R
	12					Issue List	Weekly	M	M
	11					Issue Log	As required	M	M
				32		Key Deliverable Report	Weekly	O	O
				33		Manpower Control	Weekly	O	O
			28			Manpower Estimate	Version Control	O	O
			24			Meeting & Reporting Schedule	Version Control	O	O
			25			Meeting Minutes	As required	R	R
				31		Milestone Report	Monthly	M	M
			27			Minute-by-Minute Schedule	As required	O	O
		19				Phase Plan	Version Control	M	M
				38		Post-Project Review	As required	O	R
		20				Precedence Diagram	Version Control	M	M
				35		Progress Report	Weekly	O	O

Project Inception	Project Definition	High Level Planning	Detailed Planning	Project Delivery	Project Closure	Tool	Recommended Frequency O = Optional M = Mandatory R = Recommended	Smaller	Larger
4						Project Binder	Once	O	R
	7					Project Definition	Version Control	M	M
			23			Project Meeting Agenda	Weekly	R	R
		15				Project Organisation Structure	Version Control	O	R
3						Project Start Template	As required	R	R
		18				Requirements Specification	Version Control	R	R
		22				Risk Log	As required	M	M
		20				Rough-cut Estimate	As required	O	O
5						Shaping Interview Notes	Version Control	O	R
	8					Stakeholder Analysis	As required	O	R
					40	Supplier Review	As required	O	O
			26			Task & Activity List	Version Control	R	R

Glossary of Terms

The following table lists terminology used within change management.

Term	Definition
Acceptability	The customer's feelings towards the features of a deliverable that mean it will be implemented and operated successfully.
Accountable	The state of being held to account for the quality, timeliness and cost of work for which you or another person is responsible with corresponding authority.
Activity	An element of work for which one person is responsible.
Aim	A result that your plans or actions are intended to achieve.
Aggregation	The process of combining two or more initiatives to strengthen benefits and reduce the risk of duplicating cost and effort.
Assumption	A statement of supposed fact accepted as true for the purposes of planning, which should be assessed for risk and opportunity, and replaced by a clear decision by the end of planning or if refuted converted to an issue.
Audit	An examination of the probity of a programme or project in relation to: • Regulatory requirements • Legislation • Industry standards • Organisation's quality standards.
Balanced Scorecard	An integrated set of performance measures and targets for a business.
Baselined	Indication that a document or deliverable has been 'signed-off' and can only be altered through the Change Control process.
Benefit	The measurable added value anticipated from the completion of work which can be: • Financial - having a measurable impact on the Profit & Loss Account or Balance Sheet • Non-financial – any other.
Benefit Delivery Project	A project that realises the benefits from a programme or a related group of projects.
Benefit Workshop	A facilitated meeting in which the Business Owner, Stakeholders and customer domain mangers of a programme or project: • Determine the dependencies between strategic imperatives, benefits, objectives and proposed changes • Quantify the benefits • Agree the ownership and realisation timetable of each benefit.
Business-as-usual	The day-to-day operations of the organisation that are: • Value-adding to internal and external customers • Triggered by a transaction or an event • Carried out following a process or a formula.

Term	Definition
Business Risk	A judgement first made at the outset of an initiative and then again after 'the chance of higher or lower benefit', estimated cost, contingency allowance have been determined, so that the organisation can decide if the investment is worth making.
Capability	The capacity and ability of a person or organisation to do something.
Change	An event, used to alter favourably the state of something - it involves creating, integrating or transforming the capabilities, enablers and assets of an organisation, which include people, processes and systems.
Change Framework	An end-to-end process for managing change from idea to benefit realisation, it orchestrates business-as-usual to work with initiatives and knowledge so as to realise value from change.
Change Freeze	Indication that a document or deliverable is signed-off and subject to a change embargo until a specific future date.
Change Management	The routine application of a set of processes, tools, techniques and behaviours to create a better future for an organisation – it involves creating, integrating or transforming the capabilities, enablers and assets, which include people, processes and systems.
Change Request	A necessary or wished-for modification to any aspect of a programme or project that is submitted to the Change Control process.
Chart of Accounts	An agreed list of named, numbered and budgeted areas of expenditure under which costs will be accrued for reporting purposes.
Checkpoint Activity	An activity inserted at sensing points in the Task & Activity List as a means of maintaining control.
Coach	Interacting with another in a particular context that results in improving the future for the other person.
Configuration Management	A tool used by the owner of a complex system to control implementation and change so that an audit trail is maintained and, in the event of system failure, a controlled recovery can take place with minimal disruption to business continuity.
Constraint	Physical, financial, or time limitation, or boundary within which the programme or project must proceed.
Contingency	The human, material and financial resources, and the time provisions, set aside for the execution of contingency plans.
Contingency Allowance	The actual resources set aside for the execution of contingency plans.
Contingency Plan	A scheme planned in detail for use in the event of, and to recover from, the adverse outcome of a specific risk.
Continual Improvement	Work that makes incremental improvements to business-as-usual performance which requires no significant intra-domain cooperation, uses few resources and can be authorised without escalation.
Control	Checks and balances that keep a project or programme on course to meet its agreed targets.
Cooperative Contract	A form of agreement that provides the necessary incentives to inspire a supplier to willingly, deliver on time and improve quality throughout the contract term.
Critical Success Factor	A significant entity to which achievement of objectives and realisation of benefits is critical and which must be within limits in order to achieve success.

Term	Definition
Customer Domain	A domain that implements at least one deliverable to enable planned benefit realisation.
Customer Value Proposition	A library containing information relating to target market segments, distribution channels and value propositions, including the knowledge needed to operate and support the product development environment; used to support the creation of new and revised value propositions.
Deadline	A date that if not achieved will cause the programme or project to fail.
Decision Point Activity	A scheduled activity that creates a decision about the future direction, content or structure of the programme or project.
De-commit Criteria	The circumstances under which a programme or project may be prematurely terminated.
Definition Workshop	A facilitated meeting that resolves inconsistencies and ambiguities, and unanimously agrees the project objectives and scope.
Deliverable	A change which contributes towards at least one objective, and hence the realisation of benefit, created by one domain and formally accepted by another domain.
Deliverable Workshop	A facilitated meeting involving people representing project suppliers and customers that identifies the deliverables to be created by the project at a level of detail adequate for further planning.
Development Method	A documented, systematic and proven way of completing work, used to guide the efficient creation of a complex deliverable. It: • Illustrates the major stepping stones involved in achieving the outcome • Defines the processes and interfaces between processes • Identifies the deliverables, material, equipment and quality standards.
Delivery Promise	A commitment made by an empowered person to complete agreed work in a quality manner, on time and within budget barring only unforeseen events beyond the promise-giver's control.
Dependency	A relationship which determines that an event cannot start until another event has been completed or that two or more events must start, and/or end together.
Design Specification	Illustrated designs, storyboards, drawings, models, narrative or costings that brings the concept of a complex deliverable to life at an early stage, so that it can be evaluated by prospective user or customer.
Disbenefit	A benefit to the organisation that one or more stakeholders perceive as a disadvantage to their domains.
Domain	A distinct, self-managed business unit, function, or area of expertise within an organisation that adapts to meet changing needs and demands, the performance of which is measured.
Drivers	The people or entities that forges the shape of the strategic vision, one of which one is primary.
Duration	The elapsed time needed to complete a specific activity or event.
Effort	The amount of work needed to complete a specific activity, task, phase, stage, project, or programme.

Term	Definition
Empowerment	The state of:

Empowerment — The state of:

- Understanding:
  - What work has to be done
  - How it fits in with related work
  - How all that work contributes to business needs
- Having:
  - Skills, knowledge and experience to get the work done
  - Human and financial resources to get the work done
  - Time to do own work fully and well
  - Authority to make all relevant decisions
- Being able to take responsibility for the completion of agreed work to quality, specification, time, and resource targets.

Term	Definition
Enabler	Management tool for shaping and supporting customer facing services.
Estimate	A non-binding but logically determined amount of manpower, money or time needed for the completion of a programme, project, stage, phase, task or activity.
Event	Something that takes you towards the achievement of objectives and realisation of benefits.
Exposure Assessment	A judgement made at the outset of an initiative and then again after all known delivery related risks have been assessed, mitigated, and the contingency plans produced. It is used to alert the Project Sponsor to the level of risk so that a realistic contingency allowance can be agreed. Forms part of business risk.
Feature	An attribute or characteristic of a deliverable that is expected to give an advantage and enable benefit to be realised.
Financial Benefit	Increased income, cost reduction, cost avoidance and defensive benefits that have an owner and where the strength can be measured and the difference quantified in real financial terms. Cost avoidance and defence benefits may not be allowable in a business case that examines the impact of an initiative on the organisation's profit & loss account and balance sheet.
Forecast	A non-binding judgement of the amount of manpower, money or time for the completion of work.
Forecast Date	The current expected date for completion of work, used in documents to report progress and highlight risk of slippage.
Full funding	The money and manpower granted to the Business Owner of an approved programme or project for delivery and realisation of all planned benefits.
Functionality	The features and designed actions that are necessary for a deliverable to be fit for purpose.
Functional Specification	A list of the features and designed actions that are necessary for a deliverable to be fit for purpose.
Gantt Chart	A bar-chart showing planned work over time.
Goal	A short description of the ultimate state that an organisation aspires to achieve which is perceived as an increase in value by those who have a stake in its success.

Term	Definition
Governance	The setting and enforcement of policies that legitimise activity within an environment by a panel of empowered people who delegate authority and take responsibility for the results.
Governance Gate	A point in a programme or project where feasibility and viability is reviewed and executive approval is needed before it can proceed beyond that point.
Handover	The formal transfer of responsibility from a supplier to a customer.
Heads of Agreement	The topics that need to be covered by a contract stating what you want to achieve.
Health Check	An independent study conducted on a programme or project to confirm the effectiveness of programme or project management.
Impact Analysis	The assessment of the potential impact of a project on the current internal and external domains, assets, and future capabilities of the organisation by reference to its current operating model, and Target Operating Model.
Implementation	The introduction of a deliverable into business-as-usual and making it operational.
Initial funding	The money and manpower granted to the Business Owner of an approved programme or project for: <ul><li>Early business analysis and design</li><li>Essential research and consultancy</li><li>Project Inception, Project Definition High Level Planning and Benefit Planning in the case of a project</li><li>Programme Inception, Strategy Communication, Pathfinding and Business Case creation in the case of a programme.</li></ul>
Initiative	Work that changes business-as-usual which: <ul><li>Makes an identified contribution to the organisation's strategy and business plan</li><li>Requires resources or intra-domain cooperation beyond any one person's or team's limits of authority</li><li>Has a specified beginning and end</li><li>Realises measurable benefits</li><li>Is delivered by programmes and projects.</li></ul>
Inspection	An unscheduled examination of the compliance of a programme or project in relation to: <ul><li>Regulatory requirements</li><li>Legislation</li><li>Industry standards</li><li>Organisation's quality standards.</li></ul>
Interdependency	A relationship which determines that: <ul><li>An event cannot start until an event in another initiative has been completed</li><li>Two or more events each in different initiatives must start and/or end together.</li></ul>
Internal Rate of Return	The discount or interest rate at which the net present value of an investment is zero.

Term	Definition
Investment Appraisal	The process of assessing the commercial worth of an initiative based on specific investment criteria determined by the organisation (see Bid).
Investment Budget	The discretionary spend allocated for the management and delivery of programmes and projects.
Investment Criteria	The specific factors determined by the organisation to measure the commercial worth of an initiative.
Invitation to Tender	A formal invitation to a number of potential suppliers to respond to a customer's specification of requirements - both the customer's specification and the supplier's response are binding.
Issue	An unexpected circumstance or refuted assumption that will cause slippage to a current or imminent event unless it can be resolved.
Iteration	A single cycle of work and quality assurance aimed at the creation of a deliverable.
Key Competency	The set of behaviours associated with high performance in a particular role.
Key Deliverable	A deliverable that is pivotal and for which progress towards a deadline is to be reported - when complete enables the realisation of specific benefit.
Key Performance Indicator	A measurable parameter, relevant to the organisation, which can be used to monitor progress towards its goal.
Knowledge	What is known by people and possessed by the organisation which enables constructive activity.
Knowledge Library	An organised store of intellectual assets, managed by the Change Office and available to all people doing initiative-related work.
Large-scale Project	A project of such size, complexity or duration, that success may require the use of programme management processes and separately led projects.
Leadership	Leadership is a function of knowing yourself, having a vision that is well communicated, building trust among colleagues and taking effective action.
Letter of Agreement	A simple and binding form of contract from a supplier.
Mandatory Change	A legal, regulatory, statutory or group holding company requirement to complete an initiative, such that the initiative outranks any other with a higher measured value to the organisation.
Manpower	The requirement for the effort of people to complete a programme or project.
Market Research	The process of determining need or stimulating awareness so as to establish that there is a customer demand, and a sustainable business case.
Master Project	A project within a programme that is managed by the Programme Manager to drive the programme management processes and expedite the completion of the constituent projects.
Meeting	A gathering of empowered people with an agreed purpose and agenda, who review options and reach decisions.
Mentor	Giving direct advice, when invited, by asking questions that improve a person's skills and abilities.

Term	Definition
Method	A collection of principles, processes, guidelines, tools and techniques used within a particular discipline or field of activity.
Methodology	A system of principles, processes, guidelines, tools and techniques that describe both what has to be done and how to do it.
Milestone	An identified, major point in time when a phase within a project must end in order for the project to meet its deadline.
Minutes	An agreed record of decisions, promised actions and issues.
Mitigating Action	Work that could be done before or during an event that will reduce the probability or lessen the impact.
Model	Initial design and prototyping of a deliverable.
Model Environment	A temporary physical environment created to enable the customer to experience a prototype of a deliverable so that they can accurately assess its functionality, usability and acceptability.
MoSCoW Analysis	Must have, Should have, Could have, Would like – a way of rationalising deliverables and specification functionality – it is often possible to de-scope and reduce cost without compromising quality or realisation of benefit.
Natural Duration	A fixed length of time required for the creation of a deliverable irrespective of the application of any additional resource.
Net Present Value	The future stream of benefits and costs converted into equivalent values today.
Node	An undated event on a Precedence Diagram that marks the beginning or end of a phase of a project and will become a milestone when dated.
Non-financial Benefit	A measurable improvement that is judged to make a real contribution to the effective operation or stability of the organisation but will not directly improve the organisation's profit & loss account or balance sheet.
Objective	A targeted achievement of a project or programme aimed at the initiative purpose and against which it will be measured. Objectives should be SMART: Specific; Measurable; Achievable; Relevant; Time bound.
Operating Cost	The money required by the organisation for its business-as-usual operations.
Operational Proving	The creation and testing of successive versions of deliverables so they demonstrably meet the user requirements of functionality, usability, and acceptability.
Opportunity	The chance of an event having a favourable outcome so enabling further benefit.
Organisation	Any public or private limited company, any agency or established body of national or local government, any partnership, trust or charity.
Panel	A group of people empowered to validate and assess proposed changes, take decisions and monitor benefits, within their agreed sphere of responsibility.
Pay-back Period	The point in time where it is expected that the benefits realised from an initiative will exceed the costs incurred.
Phase	A group of tasks ending at a milestone within a project.
Pilot	A full-scale test of the release version of a solution in a representative situation with real volumes to prove it to the customer.

Term	Definition
Pinchpoint	A resource centre where there is a current or imminent shortage of facilities or of people with key skills or subject matter expertise.
Plan	A detailed scheme for attaining an objective, it is used to know when you are deviating from plan so that you can either get back on plan or re-plan.
Planning Horizon	A time period for which plans will be made.
Policy	A management ruling that tells people what they can do.
Post-Implementation Review	Work within Value Management, carried out after an agreed period following the completion of a key deliverable or closure of a project or programme, to report the degree to which the stated benefits have been realised.
Post-Programme Review	Work, which is carried out just prior to programme closure to report achievement in relation to the success criteria defined in the Overall Programme Definition.
Post-Project Review	Work, which is carried out just prior to project closure to report achievement in relation to the success criteria defined in the Project Definition.
Prime Measure	The most appropriate measure of a critical success factor.
Programme	Benefit-driven work that delivers large-scale change to business-as-usual through the coordination of a coherent set of projects. It may: • Involve complex supplier and customer relationships, and deliverables • Carry significant business risk and be sensitive to many factors • Require business-wide commitment and persistence to succeed • Realise benefits in many domains • Be of long duration, usually greater than one year.
Programme Management	The agile and adaptable application of a set of processes, tools techniques and behaviours to define, plan, and deliver a large scale, beneficial change to an organisation.
Project	Work that changes or determines the path to change business-as-usual which includes: • Definition and agreement of the objectives and scope of the work • Specification of the deliverables, and their associated quality standards, that constitute the change • Planning the work of supplier and customer domains to make and implement these deliverables • Managing the issues and risks inherent in making the change • Validation and agreement of the costs and benefits • Management of change requests • Ensuring that all deliverables are created in a quality manner, on time and within budget to enable the planned benefits to be realised.
Project Community Website	An intranet site, maintained by the Change Office, providing a one-stop, self-service shop for the organisation's programme and project information.

Term	Definition
Project Management	The pragmatic application of a set of processes, tools, techniques and behaviours to deliver a beneficial change to an organisation - it involves the definition, planning and control of human, financial, material and knowledge resources; to complete the project work successfully, and so enable the realisation of planned benefits.
Project Portfolio	The record of all registered initiatives within an organisation aimed at implementing the strategy and business plan in line with its Target Operating Model, each of which realises needed benefit.
Proposal	A supplier's response to a customer's Request for Proposal, setting out: • Background, supplier overview and customer specified requirement • The features, advantages and benefits of their products and services • The supplier's capabilities and ability to meet the customer's specific requirements • An estimate or quotation • An implementation schedule.
Prototyping	The creation successive pictures, physical models and working versions of a deliverable to reveal any modifications which may be necessary prior to operational proving.
Quality	Services and deliverables that, in the opinion of the customer, are: • Fit for intended purpose • Defect free within agreed tolerances • Value for money.
Quality Assurance	The independent review by a relevant person of a deliverable or other result of work against its agreed specification and quality standards in time for any identified deficiencies to be corrected.
Quality Assurance Checkpoint	A scheduled activity within a project for carrying out quality assurance.
Quality Assurance Workshop	A facilitated meeting of relevant individuals to review a deliverable against its specification and quality standards, and unanimously agree its deficiencies in time for them to be corrected.
Quality Control	Tools and techniques used to ensure that a deliverable conforms to its specification and complies with relevant quality standards.
Quality Standard	Specific parameters or definitions by which the quality of a deliverable can be assessed: • For compliance with statutory, regulatory, legal, or industry standards • To mitigate risk • To attain accreditation.
Quotation	A firm estimate from a supplier that has a legally binding standing.
Ranking	Establishing the order in which initiatives contribute to strategy.
Regression	A return to an earlier step in the development, testing and operational proving of a deliverable made necessary by the identification of a complex deficiency.

Term	Definition
Release Management	The process used to minimise the disruption of implementing a range of improvements to a complex operating environment by marshalling together number of deliverables from separate projects and implementing them at one time, on the most appropriate and least disruptive date.
Request for Information (RFI)	An invitation to possible suppliers to provide relevant information about their organisation, its products and services, and how it does business; it is used to identify realistic contenders that are suited to the organisation's culture.
Resource	The means used to complete work including: • People's knowledge, skill, experience and time • Materials, services and equipment • Money to procure these services of people, materials, use of services and use of equipment.
Resource Management	The policies, processes, standards and practices that enable the resources of an organisation to be optimally deployed so that more can be accomplished with less resource.
Responsible	The state of being accountable with corresponding empowerment.
Review	An examination of the conduct and performance of a programme or project, at any time, in relation to: • The Bid, Project Definition or Overall Programme Definition • Organisation's project management and programme management processes and quality standards.
Risk	The adverse outcome of a future event that is subject to chance and which threatens achievement of objectives, and realisation of benefits.
Risk Assessment	The process of determining exposure of events to chance so that the risk of an adverse outcome can be determined and managed.
Risk Avoidance	An action within a programme or project that eliminates a risk.
Risk Evaluation	The process quantifying the probability and impact of a risk so that it can be managed in relation to its severity.
Risk Workshop	A facilitated meeting of relevant experts to determine the severity of risks associated with an event within a project and to generate appropriate mitigating actions and contingency plans.
Roll-out	The implementation of a proven deliverable in multiple environments.
Schedule	A plan in which quantified items are fixed within a timetable.
Scope	The boundaries, dimensions and interfaces of a programme or project that clearly identify what is included, and what is excluded.
Segmentation	The division of a programme into workstreams and projects to form its Implementation Schedule or the division of a large-scale project into consecutive or parallel smaller projects.
Sensitivity	A factor to which the outcome of an event is sensitive that may be: • Controllable - in which case the work to control it must be in the project plan • Uncontrollable - in which case it is the source of a risk to delivery and the chance of higher or lower benefit.

Term	Definition
Sensitivity Analysis	Identification of the sensitivities associated with an assumption, hazard or event to determine the: • Critical success factors • Risks to delivery • Chance of higher or lower benefit.
Service Agreement	A formal contract between a customer and supplier, usually within the same organisation.
Shape	The Sponsor's view of the domains impacted and the Stakeholders and the agreed: • Approach to planning • Required levels of reporting, monitoring and control • Reviews required • The identity of people who can authorise expenditure.
Sizing	A systematic approach to quantify the complexities and risks of an initiative.
Slippage	The amount of time, money or manpower over and above that estimated for completing a project phase, brought about by an issue.
Specification	The process of describing the functionality, usability and acceptability expected from the implementation and operation of a deliverable, in support of the conceptual and technical design.
Sponsor	A general term for a Programme Sponsor or a Project Sponsor.
Stage	A partition of a programme or project at the end of which benefits are enabled and a decision taken to proceed, alter course or terminate.
Stage Review	An assessment of the viability of a programme or project in relation to the success criteria defined in the Overall Programme Definition or Project Definition, and the Business Case or Cost Benefit Analysis.
Staging	The partitioning of a programme or large-scale project into stages, typically of 90 days duration.
Stakeholder	A person, team or domain that only has the power to influence the outcome of a programme or project.
Standard	An approved design against which others are judged or measured.
Storyboard	A simple, inexpensive series of diagrams used to clarify a deliverable and speed its development.
Strategic Imperative	One of the topics that are presently the primary focus of the organisation and which is an essential requirement of delivering its strategy.
Strategic Programme	The major transformation of an organisation, or delivery of a large-scale change to business-as-usual upon which the very survival of the organisation is dependent.
Strategy	A statement of where the business intends to go.
Straw-man	A prototype of a deliverable that is quickly and cheaply assembled to enable people to add their suggestions for change and improvement.
Successful Project Management	An agile and flexible project management methodology aimed at realising benefit from change.
Supplier Domain	A domain that deploys resources to make at least one deliverable.

Term	Definition
Supplier Review	An assessment of the quality of the relationship between an organisation and a supplier, and of the performance of that supplier, used to identify areas to be improved.
Target Operating Model	A set of charts that define the future business and technical capabilities of the organisation, and are used to guide its development.
Task	A set of closely related activities that specifies a distinct piece of work within a phase.
Team	A self-directed group of people who, together, are accountable for reaching agreed objectives and delivering agreed results.
Technical Specification	A description of the specific technical environment in which a deliverable must operate.
Template	A pattern that is used for the production of another entity.
Tender	A supplier's legally binding response to a prospective customer's Invitation to Tender, setting out:

- The details of the supplier and supplier contact information

- Features, advantages and benefits of their products, services

- Supplier's capabilities

- The supplier's ability to meet the customer's specified requirements

- Prices and discounts

- A tender price, which is a quotation

- An implementation schedule

- Any other relevant information.

Term	Definition
Terms of Reference	The definition of the objectives and scope of a complex task to be completed within business-as-usual.
Testing	The checking of functionality, usability and acceptability of a deliverable by people with different vested interests against its specification and quality standards to identify the deficiencies to be corrected in the next iteration.
Threat of Inaction	The consequences if an initiative is not advanced that should be taken into account in the assessment of the Bid.
Time Fence	A boundary created so that a conflict of interest can be escalated to a level within the organisation where there is sufficient authority for it to be resolved.
Tracking Checkpoint	A date at which progress is checked to confirm that definition and planning is proceeding to a pre-agreed timetable.
Usability	The customer's perception of the features of a deliverable that make it adequate for the purpose it was intended.
Value	A range of financial and non-financial benefits.
Value Proposition	A specification, including customer experience, product, channel, pricing and communication dimensions, describing for a related group of customers with similar needs, what they will experience when transacting business with the organisation.
Version Control	A method of numbering editions of deliverables to avoid confusion when building iterations or when making corrections and changes.
Vision	A holistic view of the way an organisation or domain must operate in order to achieve its strategy.

Term	Definition
Workshop	A facilitated gathering of relevant experts with a declared aim or objectives, used to collect ideas and information or arrive at recommendations.
Workstream	A sub-division of a programme containing a family of projects that need common oversight, direction and accountability.

Index

© Verdandi Limited 1984-2010